GOPAL KRISHNA GOKHALE

HIS LIFE AND SPEECHES

GOPAL KRISHNA GOKHALE

HIS LIFE AND SPEECHES

JOHN S. HOYLAND

GYAN

Published by

Gyan Publishing House
5, Ansari Road
Daryaganj, New Delhi-110002
Phone: 011-47034999, 9811692060
E-mail: books@gyanbooks.com

Distribution Network
gyanbooks.com
India, USA, Canada, UK, Australia

ISBN: 978-93-7169-128-4 (PB)

First Published, 1946

2nd Impression 2025

Printed at: Gyan Press, Delhi.

GOPAL KRISHNA GOKHALE: HIS LIFE AND SPEECHES
Author: JOHN S. HOYLAND

GOPAL KRISHNA GOKHALE

BUILDERS OF MODERN INDIA

Edited by S. K. RUDRA, M.A.
E. C. DEWICK, M.A.

ALREADY PUBLISHED

NĀRĀYAṆ VĀMAN ṬIḶAK. The Christian Poet of Maharashtra. By J. C. WINSLOW, M.A. Second edition.

RABINDRANATH TAGORE. His Life and Work. By EDWARD THOMPSON, M.A., Ph.D., M.C. Second edition.

PAṆḌITĀ RAMĀBĀĪ. By NICOL MACNICOL, M.A., D.Litt. Second Edition.

MAHĀDEV GOVIND RĀNAḌE. Patriot and Social Servant. By JAMES KELLOCK, M.A., B.D.

MAHĀTMĀ GĀNDHĪ. An Essay in Appreciation. By R. M. GRAY, M.A., and MANILAL C. PAREKH, B.A. Fourth Edition.

IN PREPARATION

RĀJĀ RĀM MŌHAN RĀI. By J. N. C. GANGULY, M.A., DARŚAN ŚĀSTRI.

BUILDERS OF MODERN INDIA

Gopal Krishna Gokhale

His Life and Speeches

BY

JOHN S. HOYLAND, M.A.

Y.M.C.A. PUBLISHING HOUSE
5 RUSSELL STREET
CALCUTTA
1946

To

My Student-Friends in India

1912–1928

FOREWORD

THE experience of traversing dreary wastes of other people's summarisation, in regard to Gokhale's speeches and policies, has convinced the writer of this memoir that the only adequate fashion of dealing with Gokhale is to permit him, as far as possible, to speak for himself. Consequently the following pages are filled largely with quotations from his speeches. To turn from a summary of a speech by Gokhale to the speech itself, even though it has been mutilated for reasons of space, is like turning from darkness to light; for Gokhale was not only a great orator, and a great master of clear and forcible English; but he also possessed a unique faculty of making interesting even the driest details of public business.

His speeches show a mind which was capable of undertaking laborious study of the *minutiae* of finance and statistics, but which was also possessed by a pure and undefiled zeal on behalf of the weak and oppressed, by an undying fire of love for his Motherland, and by a wideness of sympathy which made him not only a good patriot where others thought provincially or communally, but a statesman concerned with the relationships of the whole Empire, where others thought only of England or of India.

There is urgent need that this great man should come into his own, and be appreciated—especially amongst the rising generation of his contemporaries, who are now wont to dismiss him contemptuously as a 'Moderate' —at his true worth, namely, as amongst the greatest of all the builders of modern India.

The author owes a great debt to Messrs. Natesan's edition of Gokhale's Speeches; and to the work of Principal T. K. Shahani, of the Samaldas College, Bhavnagar, whose admirable monograph on Gokhale has been consulted extensively for the details of Gokhale's life. He is also much indebted to the Hon. R. P. Paranjpye's little life of Gokhale; and to a brief biography published a number of years ago by Professor J. R. Raju. He owes much also to the kindness of the Servants of India Society in Poona for the loan of the letters printed in this book for the first time. These letters, it is believed, will prove to be historical documents of some importance with regard to the genesis of the Minto-Morley Reforms of 1909. Another authority to which reference must be made is Professor V. G. Kale's *Gokhale and Economic Reforms*. I have also to thank Messrs. Venkataraman and Dravid of the Servants of India Society, Nagpur, for help received from them.

My grateful thanks are due to the Rev. Dr. Nicol Macnicol for revising the manuscript of this book, and for adding details of information arising out of his own acquaintance with Mr. Gokhale. Without Dr. Macnicol's kindly and effective help the book would never have seen the light.

June 5, 1933 J.S.H.

Note.—The Indian names occurring in this volume are given in the spelling generally familiar to English readers, without attempting to reproduce accurately the vernacular spelling by means of diacritical marks and accents.

CONTENTS

I

EARLY YEARS

Birth and Ancestry

GOPAL KRISHNA GOKHALE was born on May 9, 1866, at the little village of Katluk, in the Chiplun Taluk, Ratnagiri District, Bombay Presidency. He came of the sturdy Maratha race, which had never completely bowed before the Musalman conqueror, and which still preserved—as it does to the present day—vivid memories of the great period of Maratha revolt and independence under the national hero, Shivaji, and his successors.

Gokhale's ancestors had played an honourable part in the national history of this Maratha race. One of them had received the title of *Raste*—loyal—from the grandson of Shivaji, Prince Shahu, on account of his faithfulness in connection with certain financial responsibilities which had been entrusted to him. Other members of the family had held posts in the civil administration of the Maratha state under the Peshwas, who governed it during the eighteenth century. They were Brahmins of the Brahmins, orthodox and scrupulous in their own religious observances, and yet accustomed to deal with men of many different races, castes and types. Above all, they possessed the instinct of responsible leadership, which became so marked a characteristic of the most famous of their race. They are also said to have been men of originality and initiative, and of a generosity which sometimes placed them in considerable financial difficulties.

The father of Gopal Krishna Gokhale was named Krishna Rao Gokhale. He was educated at Kolhapur, where, by a strange chance, he was a fellow-student of the great Mr. Ranade, who was later to become his son's guide, philosopher and friend. Krishna Rao Gokhale was compelled by poverty to give up his studies, and to take a poorly-paid post at Kagal, near Kolhapur, where his high-spirited nature is said to have brought him at first into conflict with petty-minded superiors, though afterwards it won for him respect and fair treatment.

Krishna Rao Gokhale was married to the daughter of Bhaskar Pant Oka, who was a leading member of a village-community in the Chiplun Taluk of the Ratnagiri District. Although this lady had received nothing of what is usually known as education, she was a great force in her son's life. She was deeply religious, with the acute sense of the horror of sin which is characteristic of the best Hinduism. She was also a typical Hindu woman in her single-hearted devotion to her husband and her children.

Early Education

For some ten years Gopal Krishna Gokhale lived the life of an Indian village boy, in close touch with the beauties and also the ferocities of Indian nature. He became acquainted at first hand, in his most impressionable years, with the hard lot of the Indian peasant. This early experience gave him throughout his career an invaluable sense of the fundamental realities which underlie all Indian political—as well as social and economic—questions, viz. the relation of the peasant to the government, to the landlord, and to the soil which he cultivates. A large part of Gokhale's skill and wisdom, in regard especially to questions of finance and education, may be traced to the fact that he, unlike others, knew in his own person what the real India, the India of the villages, actually is and feels and thinks. However high he might rise, he was always at heart a man of the people, a member of an immemorial peasant community.

SECONDARY EDUCATION

When he was about ten years old, Gopal Krishna Gokhale was sent to Kolhapur for his secondary education, in company with his elder brother, Govind Rao. Three years later the boys' father died, and their mother was left in very straitened circumstances, with four daughters to support, as well as her two sons. It became necessary for Govind Rao to give up his education, and to take his mother and sisters to a village in another district, where a small post had been found for him, through the kindness of an uncle, on a pay of Rs. 15 a month, or about five shillings a week. However, in spite of the miserable smallness of his pay, and the responsibilities which he had to bear, Govind Rao Gokhale, who was only 18 when the change took place, managed to pay for his younger brother's education. He himself had been grievously disappointed at having to give up his studies; but he was determined that Gopal Rao should not do the same; and out of his Rs. 15 he sent monthly more than half for his brother's support. This fact is typical of the extraordinary solidarity of Hindu family-feeling. It also illustrates the value which is set upon education by the enlightened classes in India, and the sacrifices which they are prepared to make in order to obtain it.

There are a number of stories indicating the hard fight which young Gokhale had to make in order to get his education, even with this generous support from his brother. On some occasions he had even to forego one of his meals each day, in order to bring down his monthly bill in the hostel in which he lived. On other occasions he was compelled to economise by studying at night by the light of street lamps, in order to save oil. He was also obliged to do his own cooking for a time, in order to reduce his expenditure yet further, even though this involved the loss of much valuable time from his studies. All this is typical of the desperate struggle which many Indian students—probably indeed a majority of them—have to go through in order to fit themselves for their work in the world. His experiences of the hardships of a poor student's lot may be held to be partly accountable for the great value which Gokhale always placed upon education, and for the gallant fight which he made for many years in order to place it freely within the reach of every Indian boy, however poor.

College Education

Gokhale passed the matriculation examination in 1881, and went straight on to college, studying first at the Rajaram College in Kolhapur, and later at the Deccan College, Poona, and the Elphinstone College, Bombay. He was a quiet and industrious student; and both at this time and all through life showed himself to be possessed of an extraordinarily retentive memory. He is said to have learnt almost the whole of Scott's *Rokeby* by heart and to have been able at a moment's notice to give the exact context in which any difficult word is used in that book. Later on, when he became a teacher in Poona, it is said that he was in the habit of giving from memory to his class, as dictation-exercises, passages which he had casually read through in the morning paper before coming to school. It is also said that in the endeavour to train himself in the art of public speaking in English he learnt by heart *Paradise Lost* and large portions of the speeches of Burke and John Bright. The many hours which he spent in this toilsome exercise bore fruit later in the marvellous command which he possessed over the English language as a medium for clear and incisive reasoning.

Gokhale studied in the Elphinstone College at Bombay for his B.A. degree, specialising in mathematics. The teacher in this subject was Professor Hawthornthwaite, who was well known not only for his ability as an educationalist, but for the sympathetic interest which he took in his students. He is said to have held a high opinion of the young Maratha Brahman, who however only took a second class in his final examination, which he passed when only just 19 years of age. During this later period of his education Gokhale was relieved from the sense of crippling poverty which had hitherto pursued him and from the painful knowledge that his studies were imposing a cruel burden upon his brother; for he had been successful in winning a scholarship of Rs. 20 per mensem.

His Process of Self-Training

After a short period of hesitation as to whether he should take up Law or Engineering, or go to England in order to fit himself to pass the competitive examinations for the Indian Civil Service, Gokhale finally decided to make education his life-work, and took an assistant mastership in the New English High School at Poona. This was an institution which had been started five years before, in 1880, by a group of public-spirited Poona gentlemen, who were convinced that in this way they could render valuable service to their city and their country. Gokhale began work on the meagre salary of Rs. 35 per month. He found that he was faced by great difficulties in the task which he had undertaken; and it is characteristic of his thoroughness and diligence that at first he wrote out every day, and committed to memory, whatever he would have to say in the class in explanation of the English texts which he had to teach—for he began work as a teacher of English. He also learnt the texts themselves off by heart; and made a great impression upon his students by teaching Gray's *Elegy* without a book in his hand. Herein is disclosed the secret of much of his usefulness in later life—his immense capacity for taking pains for the sake of any cause to which he stood committed. He still kept up his own studies in English, as a means of fitting himself to become a good public speaker. He used to ask one of his neighbours to examine him in the passages (especially from Burke's *Reflections*) which he learnt by heart, the arrangement being that Gokhale paid his friend one anna for every mistake which he made in his recitation. It is said that the bargain proved a bad one from the point of view of the neighbour, who would sit for hours waiting vainly for even one mistake. Another plan by which he trained himself at this time was that of resolving that he would commit a certain number of pages to memory every day and then fining himself if he failed to accomplish the right number.

The result of all this self-imposed labour was that Gokhale came to have a very remarkable power of eloquent and dignified speech in the English language, whilst his memory became trained as a magnificent tool for the retention of all manner of facts and figures, and therefore as an invaluable assistant to him in his work as a statesman.

During this period of his life Gokhale was also running a coaching-establishment for students anxious to pass the Public Service Certificate Examination. In addition to this he was studying law, and kept his law terms by going from Poona to Bombay every week-end. In short, he was already showing that fierce intensity of energy which later became such a prominent feature of his character, and finally wore him out.

Out of the small salary which he received for his services as a schoolmaster, Gokhale was by now sending home more than half, in an effort to pay back to his brother, Govind Rao, some of the debt which he owed to him for his education.

He Joins the Deccan Education Society

In Poona at this time there were a number of influences tending to call a young man of character and intelligence to the service of his country rather than of himself. Foremost amongst these was the Deccan Education Society, which controlled the school in which Gokhale was teaching. Two of the members of this society, which had at that time only recently come into existence, were Mr. Tilak and Mr. Agarkar, the joint founders of the New English School. Gokhale was constantly in touch with these educationalists, both of whom had a very great influence over him, though in the case of Mr. Tilak this influence steadily decreased with the passage of the years, whilst in that of Mr. Agarkar it increased. It was largely owing to his deep respect for Mr. Agarkar that, after considerable hesitation, Gokhale finally resolved to join the Deccan Education Society. This was an act of great self-sacrifice for a young man in his position. It entailed a willingess to be content for at least twenty years with the small sum of seventy-five rupees a month (£60 a year) as allowance. The decision to join the society was therefore equivalent to a renunciation of all ambitions for wealth and prosperity. It was the taking of a kind of monastic vow. The chief obstacle in the way of this decision was the opposition of Govind Rao Gokhale, who had himself sacrificed so much in order that his younger brother might have the opportunity of becoming a great man in the world. However, once his brother's consent had been gained, and the way thus opened before him for the great step, Gokhale embraced with joy the opportunity of becoming one of a band of men who were doing so much for their country, and were deservedly held in such high esteem. He said to one of his fellow-students of law, 'You will roll in riches and drive in carriages, while I shall go on foot through life'; but he never seems to have regretted his decision; and the Deccan Education Society became for him a congenial training-ground, in which as one of a compact group of men earnestly seeking the highest good of their country, he was able to fit himself for a wider service.

Meanwhile Gokhale had been trying his hand at journalism, and in the year 1886 wrote many articles for the *Maratha*. A year or two later, having been transferred from the teaching of English to the teaching of mathematics, he published a textbook of arithmetic, which ran into a number of editions and secured the warm approval of many distinguished educationalists.

His Work in the Fergusson College

In 1884, it had been decided by the Deccan Education Society that the New English School should be developed into a college; and the first classes of the now famous Fergusson College were consequently opened, early in 1885. Before long Gokhale was teaching English in the new institution. It is recorded that at first he found considerable difficulty in mastering the nautical phraseology of Southey's *Nelson*, which was one of the books he had to teach. With his usual thoroughness he was not content till he had taken several trips to Bombay, on purpose to study the appearance and construction of the ships in the harbour, and so to fit himself for explaining these difficult matters to his students.

Gokhale remained in connection with the Fergusson College till 1904, although for the latter part of this period he was compelled frequently to be absent from Poona. Besides mathematics and English he taught at various times history and political economy, and was indeed playfully known as 'the professor-to-order.' He was willing enough to adopt such a rôle, and to serve the college by teaching whatever subject in his *repertoire* was most required; for he held strongly the opinion that in the present condition of Indian education what is chiefly needed is not specialists who have restricted themselves to the life-long study of one subject only, but all-round men who are competent to lend a hand wherever help is most required. Indeed, Gokhale never even applied the title 'Professor' to himself.

Just as his English studies had exercised a great influence upon his ability to express himself with weight and eloquence as a public-speaker, so Gokhale's mathematical proclivities served to give him that comprehensive grasp of the mathematical aspects of statesmanship, which rendered possible his great budget speeches of later years. His exactness of mind, the manner in which he understood abstruse financial questions, and his power of producing matter of fascinating interest from repulsive masses of statistics, may all be traced to the fact that for so many years he had bent his best efforts to the mastering not only of English literature but of the dry bones of mathematics.

One of his most distinguished old students records of Gokhale that as a teacher of English he was methodical in the extreme:

> 'He never slurred over even the easiest passages, and took great pains in explaining all the allusions, and especially the historical references.'[1]

Another old student says, in connection with Gokhale's lectures on Burke:

> 'Every thought of that famous political philosopher brought forth from his silver tongue a stream of illustrations chosen from the everyday life of a citizen, so that the dullest received a clear impression of the tenour of the book. To the more ambitious set of students were thrown occasional hints on higher studies in politics. . . . To have heard Gokhale lecturing on Burke's *Reflections* was to have drunk at the fountain-head of constitutionalism.'[2]

In spite of the multifarious activities in which he was engaged, Gokhale found time for various forms of recreation. As a boy he had been fond of cricket, and he

[1] R. P. Paranjpye, *Gokhale*, p. 12. [2] Shahani, *Gokhale*, p. 54.

had for long a passion for billiards. At one period he spent hours on this game every day; and he told one of his friends that when he sat out in the open on hot-weather evenings he would amuse himself by playing imaginary strokes on the stars. He was also keenly interested in chess, cards and other games, all of which he played with a characteristic intensity of concentration. The same friend, quoted above, says that on one occasion he played cards with Gokhale for fourteen hours out of the twenty-four.

Gokhale's passion for exactness was especially notable in connection with his style as a writer of English. The clearness and grace which mark his speeches are also to be seen in his letters; and it is said of him that when he had to write even the most trifling note, he would never write it hurriedly, but would always choose his words and frame his sentences very carefully, sometimes spending a lengthy period of feverish thought in search of the exact word which he required. He was extremely well-read in English literature, and his retentive memory enabled him to bring forward a wealth of quotations and illustrations with which to embellish any subject which might be under discussion, whether in the ordinary course of conversation, or in his public speeches.

In his speeches Gokhale showed a rare fluency and power of just expression, which is the more remarkable in view of the fact that he spoke generally with only a half-sheet of notepaper to guide him. His style of speaking was free from pomposity and bombast; and he impressed his hearers with the chastity of his words, no less than with the exactitude and profundity of his thought. The musical clearness of his voice was also a great asset to him.

During his career as a teacher in the Fergusson College, Gokhale seems to have impressed his students more as a teacher of history than in any other capacity. But they felt that his chief interest in the subject lay in the lessons which his mind was continually gleaning from the past for the sake of the future of his country. He would often in his lectures stray away from the matter in hand in order to discuss pressing questions of current political interest. One of his students says:

'In a course of lectures on English history he turned aside for a week to give us a résumé of the history of Ireland since the Union. The course of Irish history he always regarded as somewhat similar to that of India, and he never lost an opportunity of impressing on the minds of his pupils the long course of steady work and disinterested sacrifice which the Irish leaders have shown during the whole century. National greatness, he felt, could not be achieved in any other way. He used to take in regularly the Dublin *Freeman* and the tri-weekly edition of the London *Times*, even in his early days, to keep himself well posted in English political thought. As regards his teaching proper he read almost all the available literature on any point before he entered the class, and for the whole hour the flow of his words never stopped. . . . He did not much care for the history of India, as he thought that more lessons can be learnt from the history of Europe, both ancient and modern, which presents a well-marked evolution of the democratic idea, than from any detailed account of the numerous dynasties of rulers that ruled in India—for this, he thought, was very nearly what the history of India practically amounts to.'[1]

He was also a skilful and inspiring teacher of economics, and on this subject he entertained for a time the idea of doing some original research work, probably in connection with bi-metalism, and of publishing the

[1] Paranjpye, *op. cit.*, p. 17.

results. However in time he deliberately abandoned this idea, on the ground that his country needed his services in a broader field than that of the expert either in economics or in any other sphere of merely academic research.

His Friendship with Mahadev Govind Ranade

It was at this period of his life that Gokhale came under the influence of Mahadev Govind Ranade, the man who more than any other, not even excepting Mr. G. G. Agarkar, was responsible for his development into a great servant of India. Ranade was at this period the most distinguished of all the citizens of Poona, indeed he was often called 'the uncrowned king of Poona.' He was a man of great personal dignity and force of character, who at the same time possessed a fund of sage political wisdom which made him an admirable guide for a young enthusiast of the type of Gokhale. The cultural renaissance which during the past few years had been making itself felt in Maharashtra, and which had borne fruit in various literary and educational undertakings, as well as in a very definite stirring of the public conscience with regard to questions of social reform, was centred around Ranade, who was also an enlightened leader and thinker in regard to political and economic questions.

The first meeting between Gokhale and Ranade is said to have taken place under somewhat amusing circumstances. The New English School had on one occasion arranged a function in the Hirabagh at Poona, and had invited all the most distinguished gentlemen of the city to attend it. Gokhale was acting as doorkeeper, and had instructions to admit only those who could show tickets. Amongst others, Mr. Ranade had been invited, but when he arrived at the gate he found that he had forgotten to bring his ticket with him. Gokhale, who was not at that time acquainted with Ranade even by sight, refused to admit him. The situation was saved, however, by another gentleman who came up and, explaining matters to the conscientious doorkeeper, ushered Ranade in with all honour. This same gentleman, Aba Saheb Sathe, was afterwards the means of arranging for an interview between Ranade and Gokhale, as a result of which the latter became in a short while the devoted disciple of the great reformer.

Ranade perceived the great possibilities latent in Gokhale, and set himself to develop them, by a hard and exacting process of training, so that they might be effectively realised for the benefit of India. Gokhale for his part began to entertain an unbounded affection and respect for his *guru*, in whose presence, it is said, he would never sit down. It would be hard to discover any side of Gokhale's public activity which was not profoundly affected by Ranade's influence. For fourteen years this relationship endured, until the death of Ranade, which took place in 1901. During the first part of this time, disciple and *guru* were in constant contact, and Gokhale received a rigorous training in that industrious accuracy which marked all Ranade's work, and which was the keynote of Gokhale's subsequent success as a statesman. Ranade sent him straight to original documents; made him work through masses of Blue Books; gave him petitions and memorials to draft which entailed long and laborious research; was unsparing in his demand for articles and memoranda on all manner of subjects of public interest, which could only be mastered by the hardest and most rigorous industry.

'Under instructions from Mr. Ranade, the disciple set to work with intense application. Many were the dreary hours spent in hunting up these materials; many were the nights when sleep was denied to the young man, because work had a stronger claim. Even fever was not admitted as an excuse. "Fevers would go away if medicine were taken," the exacting master would say, "but a Wednesday lost could not be reclaimed." (Wednesday being the day when they usually met for their work). . . . Ranade never showered any praise on Gokhale in his presence, nor did he chide him if he could not approve of his productions. What he did not like he recast without any fuss. But by degrees his confidence in the young man grew; and Gokhale was entrusted with the work of drafting weighty memorials to the Government, one of which he had to finish at one almost continuous sitting of twenty-two hours.'[1]

SECRETARY OF THE SARVAJANIK SABHA

Ranade made Gokhale one of the secretaries of the Sarvajanik Sabha of Poona, which was at that time the chief political association in India.[2] This society made it its aim carefully to consider every subject of public importance which arose, and to submit the views of the people to Government in the form of lengthy and weighty memoranda, to which Government was in the habit of giving very careful attention. For a number

[1] Shahani, *Gokhale*, p. 59.

[2] 'The object of this society was to represent to Government the needs and wishes of the people, and its membership included a large number of persons of position and influence, landed-proprietors, bankers, merchants, retired Government servants, lawyers, professors, and most of the ruling chiefs of the Southern Maratha country. Ranade found in this society a means of expression for that social conscience which burned within him, and a good instrument for furthering his purposes.'—J. Kellock, *Mahadev Govind Ranade*, p. 25 (in 'The Builders of Modern India' Series).

of years the work of drafting these memoranda fell almost entirely upon Gokhale, under the superintendence and oversight of Ranade. They are written in a concise and effective style, and in a spirit of constructive statesmanship which shows how rapidly the influence of Ranade was developing in Gokhale those qualities which were to make him in later years the great force he was for nation-building.

Increased Responsibilities

During the years 1887–91, the Deccan Education Society passed through trying times, owing to differences of opinion which had arisen between Mr. G. G. Agarkar and Mr. B. G. Tilak, largely on questions of social reform, with regard to which Mr. Tilak adopted an unprogressive attitude. The situation was eventually relieved by the retirement from the society of Mr. Tilak, accompanied by Mr. Namjoshi. This for the time being greatly weakened the *personnel* of the college staff: for Mr. Tilak had been professor of mathematics and Mr. Namjoshi had performed the onerous task of the collection of funds. It was really Gokhale who stepped into the place of both these gentlemen; for he took up the teaching of mathematics which had been in Mr. Tilak's hands, and he was also called upon by his colleagues to become successor to Mr. Namjoshi as organiser and collector of the college finances. In this way, although an immense new burden was laid upon Gokhale's shoulders, he rapidly became the chief representative of the society before the eyes of the outside public; and he gained invaluable experience both of the practical management of a great institution, and of the labours and anxieties involved in all public-spirited work. He became an expert judge of men, with a wide knowledge of the manner in which they may best be approached and dealt with in order that public ends may be rightly served. He became, in other words, a tactful and accomplished leader of social, educational, and political movements. It was in this way that all through his life Gokhale's self-sacrificing readiness to undertake personal responsibility, often of a very arduous character, in connection with the causes in which he believed, became the means of fitting him for wider spheres of national usefulness. He never shirked a duty, or sought to avoid a responsibility, however busily occupied every moment of his day might be; and from each new duty and responsibility thus undertaken, he gained some fresh equipment to become a great servant of India.

As Secretary of the Deccan Education Society

The work of collecting funds for the Deccan Education Society, which Gokhale had undertaken, was no sinecure. The society had decided to erect a new building for its college. The old building in the city of Poona had to accommodate both the high school and the college classes, and was becoming impossibly overcrowded. Consequently, Gokhale set to work at the task of collecting the amount needed for the new building, devoting to this task his week-ends and his vacations. It was work of the hardest and most unpleasant character, involving a great deal of travelling, many exasperating rebuffs, and not a few disheartening experiences in regard to promises never fulfilled. However through this work Gokhale made many friendships and became one of the best known figures in Maharashtra.

The contacts thus established were afterwards of material assistance in keeping him in touch with the movement of public opinion, especially in the country districts. As a result of his untiring devotion in the cause of his college the new buildings were opened in 1895, entirely free from debt. During this period, in addition to his work as one of its professors, and as its chief collector of funds, Gokhale was secretary of the Deccan Education Society. In this capacity he had much important correspondence to carry on with Government, and many problems to solve in connection with the *personnel* of the society's workers. The constitution of the society provided for a double system of control, partly through the board of life-members, and partly through the council of the society. This dual control did not always make for smooth working; and Gokhale as secretary had many knotty problems to solve. However, in time he became not merely the trusted representative of his colleagues before the outside world, and their spokesman and protagonist in all relations both with the general public and with Government, but their guide and helper in the difficult questions of personal relationship which arose within the society itself.

As Journalist

Meanwhile, as secretary of the Sarvajanik Sabha, Gokhale was steadily accumulating political experience under the sure guidance of Mr. Ranade. The headquarters of the Sabha in Poona formed a meeting-place where citizens who were interested in public questions gathered every evening for informal discussions, which ranged over a great variety of subjects. In the same place a large amount of study was carried on, in connection with the political history of the West and its possible bearing on the future of India, and also in connection with a great variety of economic and industrial questions. Gokhale took his share in all these activities, and profited greatly by them. He had also been made responsible for the editing of the quarterly magazine conducted by the Sabha, though he had politely refused the honorarium of Rs. 40 a month which had been offered him in connection with this editorship, as he felt that it was not right to receive pay for work of this character undertaken for the sake of his country. Meanwhile, constant articles from his pen were appearing in Mr. Agarkar's Anglo-Marathi weekly, the *Sudharak*. Indeed, the English part of this paper was mainly written by Gokhale, who in this way obtained an invaluable opportunity for analysing and clearly expressing the mass of ideas regarding public questions which he was acquiring in connection with his studies under Mr. Ranade and his work for the Sarvajanik Sabha. Mr. Ranade always insisted that where his own and his lieutenants' opinions led them into conflict with the opinions held by Government, criticism must be expressed in a moderate and constructive manner; and thus Gokhale was trained to be not simply a critic of existing systems and institutions, but an organiser of something better to take their place. It was this quality of constructiveness that made him a true nation-builder in his wider activities of later life.

As Teacher

Through all these varied activities Gokhale's teaching-work in the Fergusson College went steadily forward. His students are said to have stood rather in awe of him, though he was careful to make himself perfectly accessible to them. One of them records of him:

'He spoke freely to them, and encouraged them to tell him of the difficulties that were felt by the student world. Even in the dark days of rampant extremism, there was a perceptible number of young men who remained true to the principles of moderation, mainly through the influence that emanated from Gokhale. . . . With several of the more promising students he came more intimately into contact, and gave them special personal help in their studies. . . . He was also always on the look out for promising young men to join the society as life-members, and several of us have received the first impulse towards life-membership of the society from him. Needless to say, there was no improper influencing on his part, beyond a frank discussion of all problems of the country; and the duty of spirited young men to do some public work without regard to self-interest was impressed upon them. No attempt was made to hustle them into taking the step of joining the society.'[1]

It is obvious how every element in Gokhale's environment during this early period of his manhood was converted into an opportunity for self-training in the service of his country. He was intensely eager to be of use, and his fiery energy led him to follow up one opening after another as these presented themselves before him. His character being what it was, full of self-sacrificing zeal, and marked by an indefatigable spirit of industry, whatever he laid his hand to seemed to prosper; and as the causes he advocated went forward to success, he himself was moulded by them, and by the loyal service which he gave to them, into a man who was genuinely great, because his aims lay beyond himself, and because every faculty he possessed was subordinated to his high ideals.

[1] Paranjpye, *op. cit.*, p. 22.

II

BEGINNINGS OF POLITICAL LEADERSHIP

His First Public Speech

GOKHALE'S first public speech was never actually delivered, though it brought him considerable credit. A large meeting of the citizens of Poona had been convened in order to support the action of Lord Reay in regard to a notorious case of official bribery. Lord Reay, the then Governor of the Bombay Presidency, had given an undertaking in connection with this case that any subordinate officials who gave evidence which might be incriminating to themselves should be given an amnesty from any legal penalities to which they might thus lay themselves open. The evidence given under this guarantee was, however, so damaging, and revealed a corruption so widespread, that an agitation was raised in certain quarters that some of the guilty parties who came under the amnesty should be forced to retire from public service. The Poona meeting was called in order to give evidence of the fact that public opinion supported Lord Reay, who was a very popular governor, in his refusal to go back upon his word: and also in order to deprecate any interference with the matter from England, as there had been signs that such was contemplated.[1]

[1] Shahani's account is here followed.

The ablest speech prepared for the meeting was that of Gopal Krishna Gokhale, who was then a young man of 22. It was 'taken as read' at the meeting itself; but (in accordance with what apparently became Gokhale's practice on all important occasions) it had been written out in full, and was handed to the reporters of the *Times of India* and the *Bombay Gazette*, which newspapers gave it very warm praise for its force and clearness. The affair served to bring Gokhale into public notice, with the result that in the next year (1889) he was asked to be one of the speakers at the Indian National Congress.

Work in the Indian National Congress

The Congress, which had been founded a few years previously in order to supply a means for the voicing of Indian aspirations after constitutional advance, was at this time a strictly decorous body of moderate reformers; but its deliberations were already beginning to have a definite significance for the awakening nationhood of the country; and it was a great honour for a young man of 23 to be asked to take part in them, even though at first the part assigned to him was a very minor one. However, in the Congress of 1890 he had a much more important function to fulfil, as he was asked to support the resolution on the Reduction of the Salt Duty. His speech on that occasion was the first blow struck in a long crusade, which only ended with the triumph of 1906 when the tax was reduced to a minimum figure.

From this time forward Gokhale was one of the most important personalities of the Indian National Congress. In 1892, at Allahabad, he took up the cudgels on behalf of another cause which remained a heartfelt concern with him throughout the rest of his life, namely the Indianisation of the public services. He was now rapidly becoming known throughout India as one who brought to the national cause not merely immense powers of industry and of detailed application, but a deep moral enthusiasm, which can best perhaps be compared to that which had distinguished John Bright, the great tribune of the common people of England. Gokhale was not a mere machine for the digestion of statistics and the manipulation of Blue Books; but he was one who saw the issues of national emancipation in terms of right and wrong, and who possessed the capacity for imparting to his fellow-countrymen his own ardent moral convictions on all such issues.

His Capacity for Hero-worship: Mr. Ranade

One of the great forces in Gokhale's life at this time was his capacity for hero-worship. His relations with Mr. Ranade have already been noticed. Those relations were to continue to exercise a great influence upon the younger man till Mr. Ranade's death, and were to leave a permanent impression upon Gokhale's character. In this connection it will be of advantage to quote some memorable words spoken by Gokhale on a later occasion about his friend:

'The younger men who came in personal contact with him felt as in a holy presence, not only uttering "nothing base," but afraid even of thinking unworthy thoughts while in his company. The only other man who has exercised a similar influence on me in my experience is Mr. Dadabhai Naoroji. Among Mr. Ranade's great qualities one of the most prominent was his utter, absolute unselfishness. As I have already told you, he was incessantly working in several fields, but never did he seek the least recognition, never did he think of his getting, or not getting, credit for this or that. Indeed nothing pleased him more than to do his work—not only political, but almost of every kind—from behind somebody else. His great anxiety was to get more and more men to be interested in and associated with the work. I do not think anybody ever heard Mr. Ranade say, "I did this, I did that." It was as though the first person singular did not exist in his vocabulary. The humility with which he sought to discipline himself almost to the last day of his life was another of his great qualities. By nature he was very sensitive, feeling keenly injustice or meanness in any shape or form; but his constant effort to discipline himself enabled him to preserve his calmness even under the most trying circumstances. The normal state of his mind was indeed one of quiet cheerfulness, arising from a consciousness of work well done, and from humble faith in the purpose of Providence. But even when he was seriously displeased with anything, or disappointed with anyone, or suffered inwardly owing to other causes, no one who did not know him intimately could detect any trace of that suffering on his face. And never did any one—not even those who stood nearest to him—hear him utter a word of complaint against those who might have done him personal injury. He insisted on having all attacks on him in newspapers carefully read out to him. He was constantly before the public in one capacity or another, and his views, therefore, came in for a good deal of criticism—friendly and unfriendly almost from day to day. The appreciative notices that appeared he did not always read through. I know —because I sometimes had to read the papers to him—he never read them himself, his sight being defective. But all unfriendly criticism he made a point of hearing. He wanted to know if there was any idea therein that he could accept. And in any case, even if there was pain in hearing all that was said, that pain itself had its disciplinary value.

'One more great quality of his I would like to mention, and that was his readiness to help all who sought his help—and especially those who were weak and oppressed. He was accessible to all, even the humblest, at all hours of the day. No one ever wrote to him without receiving a reply. He listened patiently to everyone, whether he was able to help or not. This indeed was to him a part of his practical religion. After the Amraoti Congress of 1897, when we were returning to this part of the country, he and I were, for one night, the only occupants of our carriage. At about 4 a.m. I was suddenly roused by some singing in the carriage and on opening my eyes I saw Mr. Ranade sitting up and singing two verses of Tukaram again and again, and striking his hands together by way of accompaniment. . . . The verses were these: "He who befriends the weary and the persecuted —he is a true saint, and God Himself is to be found there;" and, "Be you humble and seek the favour of saints. If you want to meet God, this is an easy way."

'As I sat listening to these verses, I could not help realizing how constant was Mr. Ranade's endeavour to live up to this teaching, and how simple and yet how glorious was the rule of life that it inculcated. It was a rich moment in my own life. The scene indeed will never fade from my memory.

' I have told you as briefly as I could what it was that most struck me in Mr. Ranade. I think that for about thirty years he represented our highest thought and our highest aspirations, and it will be long before we shall have another like him in our midst.'

A man's true nature is to be known from his enthusiasms. The ideals are the real man. In his unbounded love and reverence for his *guru*, as shown in these quotations, we see into the soul of Gokhale far more clearly than is possible through the reading of any number of speeches delivered by him. He was a man into whose life had come a great personal influence of goodness, self-sacrifice and devotion, a man who had seen and valued aright the worth of these things, and a man who was determined to live his own life in accordance with the ideal thus set before him.

Gopal Krishna Gokhale

Mr. Dadabhai Naoroji

Mr. Ranade's personal influence was by far the most important single element which went to the making of Gokhale; but he had other heroes upon whom he tried to model his own character. Chief amongst these was Mr. Dadabhai Naoroji, who as member for Central Finsbury in the British House of Commons did a great work in bringing the needs of India before the English people. When Gokhale was 27 years of age a great demonstration was organised at Poona in honour of Mr. Naoroji, who was then in India, and was to preside at the National Congress. Gokhale threw himself heart and soul into the work of preparing for this function, and was so eager to be of service to the great man that, as a sort of unofficial aide-de-camp, he drove to the meeting on the coach-box of the carriage in which Mr. Naoroji rode. Many years afterwards, on the occasion of the celebration of Mr. Dadabhai Naoroji's eighty-first birthday, Gokhale spoke of him as follows:

'How is it that Mr. Dadabhai Naoroji has in the course of time attained in the hearts of millions of his countrymen, without distinction of race or creed, a place which rulers of men might envy, and which in its character is more like the influence which great teachers of humanity have exercised on those whose thoughts and hopes and lives they have lifted to a higher plane? To us he is not merely a great political leader—the foremost of our time, and for the last half century. It is because he embodies in his person all that is high and noble in our land, and stands as the sacred representative of our national aspirations for the future, that our deepest devotion is given to him. He had attained this position before many of us were born, and few are those among us whose earliest awakening to the claims of nationality has not been influenced by his teaching and his example. Eighty years ago, when Mr. Dadabhai Naoroji first saw the light of day, if any one had ventured to predict that he would one day stand forth as the most trusted spokesman of a united India, such a man would have been set down as a dreamer of wild dreams. In 1825 the power of the Marathas had just been overthrown; and though the first generation of British administrators, foremost among whom will always stand the honoured name of Elphinstone, had taken in hand the work of consolidation in a spirit of wise and liberal statesmanship, the people on this side were naturally sullen and discontented, and not without a vague expectation that their own Government would return some day. Western education had then hardly begun—the Charter Act of 1833 was still some way off—and the idea of the different parts of this great country drawing together in a common feeling and a common aspiration could have been no more realised even mentally than is the idea of a united Asia realised by us today.

'I think it is to the infinite honour of British rule and the wise and large-hearted policy followed in the administration of the country—especially in matters of education—that what was then almost difficult to conceive has now already become a fact and a reality. And to Dadabhai Naoroji and the earliest band of Indian reformers that worked with him belongs the credit of understanding aright the true meaning of the new order of things and the possibilities that it implied for their countrymen, and of throwing themselves heart and soul into the work of realising those possibilities in practice. Since then one generation of workers has entirely disappeared from the scene, and of the next only a few are left—may they long remain with us!—to guide us. But Dadabhai Naoroji has all through remained in the forefront of the movement, and neither age nor disappointment has chilled his ardour, nor has absence diminished his hold on his countrymen. . . .'

It is noteworthy, with regard to both the addresses quoted above on Gokhale's heroes, that when, at the prime of his powers, the great statesman looked back upon the influences which had made him, he chose out for especial mention qualities which may be spoken of as spiritual rather than mental. It was not so much their ability as statesmen, administrators or politicians which had appealed to him, as the fact that they were marked by a type of character which he describes as 'saintly'—that in contact with their spirit he had come to acquire a higher ideal of what human nature might mean in 'purity, simplicity, gentleness, self-denial.' In the midst of all his intense political activity, and equipped as he was with a keen practical intellect, and with a magnificent capacity for hard, slogging, detailed work, there was always a deeper side to Gokhale's personality, a life of the spirit which comes to the fore on occasions such as those instanced above, where he is speaking out from his heart the meaning to him of the great men whom he looked upon as his guides and preceptors.

Mr. G. G. Agarkar

Another great formative influence in Gokhale's life was his association with Mr. Agarkar. This gentleman was not only a distinguished educationalist, but was also a social reformer of deep convictions, and a journalist who exercised a great deal of influence in the Maratha country. In this capacity he had first written for the *Kesari,* of which journal he had been the main editor; but the increasing influence of Mr. B. G. Tilak upon the *Kesari*, and his opposition to many of Mr. Agarkar's views with regard to social reform, finally led the latter to start the *Sudharak*, and to retire from his connection with the *Kesari*. In the control of the *Sudharak* he and Gokhale became very closely associated, Gokhale writing the English portion of the paper, whilst Agarkar took the major part, which was in Marathi. Gokhale's articles generally dealt with political questions, whilst those written by Agarkar were mainly concerned with social reform, on which subject he wrote with extraordinary force and cogency. Occasionally, however, Gokhale wrote the Marathi portion (he both spoke and wrote his mother-tongue excellently), whilst Agarkar wrote the English articles. The *Sudharak* had at first a hard struggle to pay its way; for in those days social reform was anything but a popular cause. Later, however, it did much better. Gokhale's connection with the paper lasted for some four years; and there can be no doubt that his close association with a man of the fearless outspokenness, and the contempt for popular prejudices which marked Mr. Agarkar, had a great influence upon the development of his character.

Social Reform

Gokhale himself did not feel able for a long time to take any leading part in connection with the movement for social reform. In his own life there had been a tragedy. Shortly after his father's death and when still a young lad, he had been married, by his uncle's instrumentality, to a girl who was afterwards found to be suffering from an incurable disease, and who could not be his real wife. His relatives pressed him to take a second wife; and after much hesitation, he consented to do so. Though he had obtained the permission of his first wife to this step, and though it was taken at a time in his life when he had apparently not begun to consider the rights and wrongs of such questions, he felt for long afterwards that this episode precluded him from taking the lead in movements for social reform. There came a time, however, when in spite of the consciousness of having thus committed, as one of his Indian biographers remarks, 'a sin against society,' he felt himself impelled to speak out strongly with regard to the treatment of the depressed classes amongst his fellow-countrymen: and to point out the inconsistency of the persistence of such treatment in view of the resentment felt throughout India towards the similar treatment of Indians in South Africa. On one occasion he gave great offence to orthodox Hindus by partaking of refreshments at the headquarters of a Poona Mission, but he paid no attention to the agitation which was raised at the time, or to the social penalties which were threatened against him.

Moreover, he was always a staunch supporter, by sympathy and personal counsel and influence, of anyone who felt called upon to take a decided stand against reactionary opinions or customs.

Relations with Mr. B. G. Tilak

It was largely with regard to questions of social reform that the famous estrangement developed between Gokhale and his notable contemporary and rival in the affections of the Maratha people, Mr. B. G. Tilak. Tilak was the older man, and Gokhale used to say that his original decision to join the Deccan Education Society and to devote his life to the service of his country had been due to his admiration for Tilak rather than to his admiration for Agarkar, though later he was destined to come into such close and cordial relationships with the latter. Tilak was a man of great personal force of character; but he was a very hard man to work with as a colleague, and his views steadily developed in a direction contrary to those of Gokhale and Agarkar, especially in regard to questions of political agitation and of social reform. After Agarkar withdrew from the *Kesari* and founded the *Sudharak*, there were frequent 'battles royal' between the two Maratha leaders in the columns of their respective journals; and matters became very strained in the Deccan Education Society, and in the counsels of the Fergusson College. It was a great relief to the other members of the society when, in 1890, as has already been recorded, Tilak decided to break his connection with it, taking with him Mr. Namjoshi. After his resignation, Tilak began rapidly to gravitate towards the orthodox side of things. This greatly increased his popularity; for orthodoxy in regard to questions of social reform was still very definitely the popular point of view. The public of Poona had distinctly sided with Tilak over the question of his resignation from the society; and he soon began to exercise an increasingly significant influence in regard to political affairs. His attitude became one of intransigent opposition to Government; and later, as is well known, he coquetted with doctrines of physical force in a manner which led eventually to his imprisonment.

The contrast between these two leaders, Gokhale and Tilak, became more and more emphasised as the years went by. Gokhale believed in social reform, and in constitutional methods for the winning of a better and freer future for his country. Tilak became more and more orthodox and extreme. In consequence Tilak was always, at any rate amongst his Maratha fellow-countrymen, the more popular figure. So in fact he remains today; but, none the less, the methods of Gokhale are the methods in accordance with which the new India is being created before our eyes.

In consequence of his popularity with the rank and file of the Hindu citizens of Poona it was generally true that on those not-infrequent occasions when a direct issue was joined between Gokhale and Tilak, the latter won what appeared to be a victory. He succeeded in capturing the Sarvajanik Sabha, by adroit manipulation of its elections. He made great capital out of Gokhale's apology to Government in connection with the affair of the 'Poona murders.'[1] He became the leader of a party in the Congress which it was increasingly difficult for Gokhale to control; and right at the end of Gokhale's life, after Tilak's return from jail, he was responsible for the so-called 'compromise controversy' which may be said to have broken Gokhale's heart. In various other relations the divergence of spirit and policy between the two leaders was made more and more definitely apparent as the years went by. Perhaps it could scarcely have been otherwise. A man of strong views who essays to lead a people still largely uneducated along the paths both of social reform and of well-consolidated constitutional advance, is bound to find that he rouses opposition on the part of those who prefer methods less radical as regards social questions, and more precipitate in the field of politics. It was Gokhale's misfortune that the protagonist of this inevitable reaction was one of his own old friends and colleagues, and a man for whom he had himself entertained in early days a deep personal admiration.

Hindu-Moslem Relationships

In no connection was the difference between these two great Marathas more marked than with regard to the perennial problem of Hindu-Moslem relationships. Tilak being both an orthodox Hindu and a strong Maratha

[1] See below, pp. 56 ff.

nationalist, became inevitably more and more definitely an anti-Moslem. The Maratha State had been built up, in the seventeenth century, on a strong anti-Moslem nationalism. In the course of constant wars, Shivaji, the founder of that State, had proved more and more conclusively his own and his people's right to repudiate all Musalman pretensions to overlordship. During the eighteenth century the Maratha armies had gone out eastward, northward and southward, to the conquest of the Musalman power. They had shattered the great Moghal Empire into pieces, and had ruled its former provinces. There had sprung up amongst them a fierce contempt for the Musalman system of religion and conduct. For a couple of generations after the British conquest, this spirit had lain dormant; but with the Maratha renaissance which came in the last two decades of the nineteenth century, it began to re-awaken. The focus of danger was the celebration of the great Muhammadan festival of the Muharram, in which an imposing procession took place through the streets of Poona. In the old days the Hindus had freely joined in the celebration of Muharram; but the rising tide of Maratha nationality made the orthodox Hindu party more and more restive at such fraternisation, and more and more insistent in their opposition to the slaughter of the cow—the Hindu sacred animal—by Musalmans.

Tilak became the protagonist of this new anti-Moslem sentiment, and began to organise and develop the worship of the Hindu god, Ganpati, in opposition to the Muharram celebrations, exhorting the Hindus to take no share in these, but to concentrate on a revived worship of Ganpati. This advice was eagerly listened to, especially by the orthodox upper classes; and it soon became apparent that the movement had in it the seeds of a dangerous estrangement between the Musalman and Hindu communities. Men of the type of Gokhale, who thought for India as a whole, and knew that the most pressing of all her problems was that of a permanent and solid reconciliation between the two communities, beheld Tilak's activities in this respect with the greatest concern.

Gokhale was always insistent upon the necessity for bringing about a good understanding between Hindus and Musalmans, of creating and fostering opportunities for their friendly co-operation, instead of emphasising their differences. He strongly opposed all attempts to create a Hindu class-consciousness in opposition to Islam. The gulf was already wide enough. The memories of ancient conflicts must be allowed to die. Every agency must be encouraged which enabled Hindus and Musalmans to work together harmoniously for the good of India as a whole.

Here again Gokhale was taking the unpopular side, and of necessity found himself more and more definitely estranged from his old colleague.

If Ranade, Naoroji and Agarkar acted as great positive influences in Gokhale's development (and to these must be added another famous name, that of Sir Pherozeshah Mehta, the Parsi leader for whom Gokhale always entertained a profound admiration, and with whom he declared he would rather stand alone than be in agreement with the rest of the world) Tilak formed an almost equally decisive influence of a negative significance. The two men seemed to be driven asunder by a disruptive force. Increasing extremism on the part of Tilak led to a deeper realisation of the meaning and value of constitutionalism on the part of Gokhale.

Beginnings of Political Leadership

As Tilak's orthodoxy grew more narrow, so Gokhale perceived more clearly the necessity for basing India's welfare upon a genuine and widespread development of liberal-mindedness, enlightenment and sterling character. As Tilak found himself emphasising more and more the ideal of Maratha nationality, founded upon a revival of opposition to Islam, Gokhale found himself compelled more and more energetically to plead for a comprehensiveness of spirit which should be willing to sink all communal differences on behalf of Indian nationality. As Tilak centred his orthodoxy of Hindu belief, and his revival of the Maratha spirit, around a new symbolism, in the worship of the image of Ganpati, Gokhale was more and more effectually impressed with the need for dispensing with such symbolism, and for making the Congress—and later the new Councils of the Minto-Morley reforms—the real focus of Indian nationality. Finally, as Tilak's popularity grew amongst the rank and file of a people still largely uneducated, Gokhale perceived ever more clearly the emptiness of mere popularity — which he was too great a man ever to covet for its own sake—and the supreme necessity of a widespread system of popular education.

III

THE WELBY COMMISSION, AND AFTER

Gokhale's Political Principles

ATTENTION has already been drawn to the fact that Gokhale deliberately turned his back upon popularity. His opponents of the Tilak school had a great popular following which they attracted and retained by methods of which he did not approve. He might have fought them with their own weapons; but in this case he would have had to sacrifice his principles, and this was impossible for him.

'Mainly on account of the methods of propaganda which were followed by Mr. Tilak, and which Gokhale and his followers have never cared to follow, Gokhale has never been a popular hero in Maharashtra. Of course he had always his band of faithful followers who remained attached to him through thick and thin, and whose attachment was a source of great comfort to him. . . . He hated shams of every kind, and this is why he spoke equally strongly on the defects of Lord Curzon's administration, or on the outrageous treatment of Indians in South Africa, and on the Indians' attitude to the depressed classes in their own country. He realised that nine-tenths of the work that has to be done before India can take her rightful place in the British Empire and the world, must be done in India and by Indians themselves: and that when this major part of the work is accomplished, the few difficulties necessarily inherent in a foreign bureaucratic government will not take long to get over. Such an acute sense of one's own shortcomings is inconsistent with a readiness to shout with the biggest crowd. He often used to say that. . . . the great task before us is to try and raise the average level of Indians. Hence Gokhale's admirers were mainly the *élite* of the land, who could be approached by an appeal to their judgment; and perhaps the appreciation of him was more widespread outside than inside the Bombay Presidency, as the general vision is more likely to be obscured on a nearer view by the action of merely local obstacles. Gokhale was thus essentially a man of India rather than a man of Poona or even of Bombay.'[1]

One of Gokhale's main political principles—and one which brought him into acute disfavour with the 'extremists'—was his insistence on the necessity to India of the British connection. His aim was not an India independent of the British Empire, but Dominion Status within that Empire. This was the end for which he continually laboured. In the middle years of the nineteenth century, Dominion Self-government had been rapidly and generously extended to the English-speaking colonies of the Empire. The time had now come, in his belief, for the beginnings of a similar movement in regard to the great Eastern dependency. In the nature of things it was an end to be attained by constitutional methods, by education of Indian opinion, by making the most of every avenue open to the expression of that opinion, by practical demonstration of the fact that Indians were capable of responsible government, and by the painstaking manipulation of all legitimate means by which pressure might be brought to bear, both upon the Indian and the English governments, for the liberalising of constitutional machinery in India.

This method of working demanded immense patience,

[1] Paranjpye, *op. cit.*; p. 34.

and involved crushing disappointments. It involved a two-fold movement, proceeding simultaneously—that of the extension of enlightenment and the development of character on the one hand, and that of constitutional advance on the other. Both were in the nature of the case slow processes. There was no swift and easy road to the millennium of independence. The boon must be deserved.

It is easy to see that such an outlook was not calculated to appeal to the ardent nationalists whose numbers were rapidly increasing all over India. Especially to the students, and above all, to the students in his own homeland of Maharashtra, it seemed (as it still seems) that Gokhale's method was insufferably tedious; that it involved an undignified dependence upon English clemency; that it was inconsistent with the dignity of a great people, whose traditions of victorious independence lay in the still recent past.

Yet Gokhale never abated his insistence upon these twin principles—that advance must be constitutional advance, deserved through the spread of enlightenment and education; and that the British connection was essential to the well-being of India.

Again, as has already been noticed, Gokhale insisted, in season and out of season, upon the necessity of the Hindus carrying the Musalmans with them in their growing national consciousness and demand for freedom. Good feeling and cordial co-operation between the two communities was the only basis upon which a sound and united national life could be built up. This was bitter doctrine to the advanced political school, who 'played upon the imagination of the ignorant and superstitious, depicting the horrors of contamination with the Moslem, which the liberal-minded "Moderates" were said to recommend.'[1]

In regard to his relations with the Government, Gokhale stood first for a careful and thorough use of all the constitutional machinery already available for bringing Indian opinion to bear upon Government policy. In the second place he kept a vigilant eye upon administrative detail, and was insistent upon the necessity for reform and redress, whether in a general financial policy, or in any matter of official high-handedness, as for instance with regard to the partition of Bengal. The immense pains which he took in working up his facts and figures, and in substantiating his position in every possible way, especially with regard to his great Budget speeches, made him far more than a mere leader of opposition in the Legislature. Though he never held any responsible office as a legislator, he was known to be a genuinely constructive statesman, whose criticisms were to be welcomed in the same spirit in which they were offered, as an honest attempt to help the Government to discharge its obligations to India in the right manner.

Thus when Gokhale pressed for constitutional reform, his opinions and advice carried immense weight, above all in his insistence that reform should be generously offered, rather than conceded under compulsion. His attitude may be indicated by a passage from one notable speech:

'The Government will no doubt put down—indeed it must put down—all disorder with a firm hand. But what the situation really requires is not the policeman's baton or the soldier's bayonet, but the statesman's insight, wisdom and

[1] Shahani, *op. cit.*, p. 79.

courage. The people must be enabled to feel that their interests are, if not the only consideration, at any rate the main consideration, that weighs with Government, and this can only be brought about by a radical change in the spirit of the administration. Whatever reforms are taken in hand, let them be dealt with frankly and generously. And let not the words, "too late," be written on every one of them. For while the Government stands considering, hesitating, receding, debating within itself, "to grant or not to grant, that is the question"—opportunities rush past it which can never be recalled. And the moving finger writes, and having writ, moves on.'[1]

These noble words were followed by the granting of the Morley-Minto reforms, which may be regarded as due in no small measure to Gokhale's influence and to the warnings which he had uttered. Still more were the Montagu-Chelmsford reforms, which came ten years later, a concession to his spirit of sane and liberal statesmanship, and a memorial to his constructive workmanship. He would not have approved of all aspects of those reforms. He would have considered them dangerously delayed; and he would have been outspoken in his denunciation of the tragic events of 1919 which reacted so disastrously upon the fashion in which the new constitution was received in India. None the less those reforms in themselves, and above all when considered as an instalment of future self-government, are a real measure of the national usefulness of Gokhale's life-work.

Sir William Wedderburn wrote thus of Gokhale:

'In no case did he fail to produce a profound and favourable impression by the accuracy of his information and the cogency of his arguments. At personal interviews he was

[1] The concluding words of Gokhale's Budget speech of 1908.

equally successful. To the credit of British statesmen of all parties it must be recorded that they have all been willing to give a hearing to Mr. Gokhale, and it is no secret that, as Secretary of State for India, Lord Morley accorded to him prolonged interviews, at which he set forth fully the needs and aspirations of the Indian people. The information thus imparted influenced in no small degree the concessions granted in the Morley-Minto reforms.'[1]

These words serve to bring out one of the most important of Gokhale's principles in regard to his work for his country—that work must be done thoroughly. He gave unsparingly of his time and efforts to the investigation of the causes in which he was concerned, and to the working up of all available evidence regarding them. He was effectually aided in this task, on the one hand by his marvellous memory, and on the other by the rigorous training which he had received under Mr. Ranade during the period when, as secretary of the Poona Sarvajanik Sabha, he had been employed in working up cases to be presented to Government in regard to various public questions. But memory and training were only tools employed by the man's own personality—by his indomitable will, which refused no sacrifice of comfort or leisure for a cause he believed in, and by his character of thoroughness, of honesty, of persistent diligence.

Secretary of the Congress

These then were the principles which Gokhale brought to his public work. The first important task laid upon him with regard to the organization of public opinion was the secretaryship of the Bombay Provincial Conference,

[1] Quoted from the *Daily News* by Shahani.

which he held in 1893 and 1894. He acquitted himself so well in regard to this arduous and thankless piece of work that he was given the honour of being made one of the secretaries of the National Congress, which was held at Poona in 1895. The arrangements for a congress entail the finding, or building, of accommodation for many thousands of guests, the erection of an immense 'pandal,' or temporary hall of assembly, the settling of ten thousand details regarding the food, the drink, and the comfort generally of the delegates, and above all the collection of a very considerable amount of money, whereby all these various expenses may be met. Gokhale brought to the task all his accustomed energy and capacity for detail; but he found himself hampered at every turn by the influence of the 'extremist' school which has been referred to above, and which at this period was showing not merely indifference but actual hostility to the Congress, mainly on the ground that the Congress had become identified with the cause of Social Reform, to which they were bitterly opposed. This hostility crystallised into a demand that the All-India Social Reform Conference, which in recent years had been allowed to hold its sittings in the 'pandal' of the Congress, should be deprived of this privilege, and should be compelled to make arrangements for its accommodation elsewhere. Eventually, in spite of the fact that this pettifogging point of view was by no means generally entertained, it was decided by those responsible for the Congress that the concession should be made; and, in consequence, a very great deal of additional work was rendered necessary, as a separate place of assembly had to be erected for the use of the Social Reform Conference.

The Welby Commission, and After

In other respects also the 'extremist' party made Gokhale's work very difficult; for example, by their efforts to pack the Reception Committee. They are said even to have descended to threats of physical force. It actually became needful to begin the issue of a new journal, the *Rashtra Sabha Samachar*, in order to counteract the influence of the *Kesari*; and Gokhale was responsible for writing this.

The unpleasant experiences connected with his work as secretary of the Congress of 1895 were in the long run of much benefit to Gokhale, in training him in the management of men, and in the administration of a great political undertaking. They may also have had much to do with the development in him of that admirable faculty for differing from his opponents in a courteous and amiable manner which marked him in later life.

In 1896 the reactionaries succeeded in capturing the Sarvajanik Sabha; and a year later their methods brought them into conflict with Government, as a paid lecturer appointed by them had made some rash assertions, which were neither explained nor withdrawn. Consequently Government passed an order to the effect that the representations of the Sabha, which had been of such service in the past, could no longer be considered. Some time before this happened, however, Gokhale had resigned his secretaryship of the Sabha, since he found it impossible to work under the new conditions, and with the help and advice of Mr. Ranade had started a new society, the Deccan Sabha, which continued the constructive type of work which had been carried on for so long by the Sarvajanik Sabha.

The Welby Commission

It had been increasingly impressed during the past few years upon Gokhale's mind that the right programme of constitutional advance for India lay along the line of a progressive association of Indians in the control of the country's finances. He perceived how intimately in the history of England the development of democratic institutions had been connected with the enforcement of the people's claim to a voice in the disbursement of the taxes which they paid. He perceived also the immense force which had been given to the cause of American liberty by the appeal to the maxim, 'No taxation without representation,' a maxim which was in itself a revival of an ancient constitutional principle of English history. These convictions led Gokhale to throw himself with increased energy into the study of the problems of Indian finance, from every possible point of view; and in co-operation with Rao Bahadur G. V. Joshi, who was an expert economist, he soon made the Deccan Sabha a notable instrument for the spreading of enlightened interest in financial affairs. In his public speeches on the Congress platform and elsewhere Gokhale also gave abundant proof of his thorough-going grasp of Indian economic problems. In 1896, a Royal Commission was appointed, presided over by Lord Welby, in order to enquire into the financial relationships of India and England; and public bodies in India were invited to send their representatives to London in order to lay their views before the Commission, which did not itself visit India. The Deccan Sabha decided to accept this invitation; and as neither Ranade nor Joshi could themselves go to England, the task of laying the Sabha's views before the Welby Commission fell upon Gokhale, who was then only 31 years old. He made the most of this opportunity, spending three months in a concentrated endeavour to make his evidence before the Commission as comprehensive and convincing as it could possibly be. When he felt himself prepared, Mr. Ranade put him through the most searching cross-examination, taking up the official point of view for this purpose, as the Commission itself was largely composed of redoubtable official experts. After a rigorous test Ranade pronounced himself satisfied with his pupil's equipment; and Gokhale embarked for England, in the company of Mr. (later Sir) D. E. Wacha, who was also to give evidence before the Commission, and to whom he soon became greatly attached.

Economic Problems

Gokhale duly appeared before the Commission, and was heard for two whole days. His evidence, which was delivered in a manner at once both cogent and profound, made his reputation as one of the foremost Indian economists and statesmen. His general attitude to the financial problems of his country may be summed up in the following sentence from his evidence:

> 'Whereas the capacity of the country to bear increased burdens is growing perceptibly less, our expenditure, under the existing conditions of administration, is rising higher and higher, necessitating a heavy incidence of taxation, exhausting all our fiscal reserves, and, what is still more alarming, thrusting on our hands expanding responsibilities.'

He was firmly convinced that the revenue of India, depending as it did very largely upon the land tax, was of a fundamentally inelastic character; and he also held that the salt tax, which formed the most important source of revenue next to the land tax, was not only incapable of being made to yield more revenue, but was 'the highest tax that has ever been imposed upon a prime necessity of life,' and called urgently for reduction. He urged therefore that the expenditure of the Indian Government should be adjusted to the fact of this inelasticity of income—or at least to the fact that income could only be expected to expand with the normal growth of the population, and with definite improvement in Indian conditions of life. He pointed to the terrible famines which were experienced in India as proof of the fact that the country was incapable of bearing increased financial burdens, and indeed that the burdens already imposed upon her were too heavy for her strength. He regarded the proceeds of the income tax and the salt tax as the only trustworthy indication of the real financial position of India, and maintained, both in 1897 and later, that neither of these was showing any decided increase, the second even failing to keep pace with the normal growth of population. Hence he concluded that both the upper and the middle classes, whose state of prosperity is shown by the proceeds of the income tax, and the masses of the population, whose position is indicated by the salt tax, were in anything but a satisfactory condition economically. Increase of revenue under land tax he refused to regard as indicative of increased prosperity, since the people were forced to pay the enhanced taxation under this head on pain of parting with their land. Increase under excise merely showed that drunkenness was more prevalent than formerly; and the increase under the heading of 'stamps' merely showed that the people were becoming more litigious.

The Welby Commission, and After

It cannot be denied that the series of devastating famines which occurred in India at the end of the nineteenth century lent considerable weight to Gokhale's often-repeated contention that the material condition of the masses of the Indian population was deteriorating, rather than improving. He was never tired of drawing attention to this phenomenon, 'the saddest in the whole range of the economic history of the world.' His position is thus summed up by one of his Indian biographers:

> 'That a peasantry inferior to none in industry, frugality and patient suffering should, at the end of half a century of an uninterrupted peaceful rule, find itself in a worse plight than it has ever been in, was a painful fact demanding the earnest and immediate attention of Government, which could best be focussed by having a formal investigation made, where the non-official student of the subject should be invited to co-operate with official representatives.'[1]

As time passed, and the period of famines was succeeded by one of increasing prosperity, Gokhale ceased to urge his thesis that the people of India were actually becoming poorer; but he never till the end of his life ceased to insist upon the necessity for rigorous economy, or to protest against any indication that the Government of India were tending to overlook the very narrow limits within which any projected attempt to increase the revenue must be confined, owing to the peculiar inelasticity of the sources of taxation.

Expenditure on the Army

With regard to the details of his evidence before the Welby Commission, Gokhale drew especial attention to

[1] Shahani, *op. cit.*, p. 110. Shahani is especially valuable with regard to Gokhale's views on economic problems.

the expenditure on the Indian army, and in this connection made the following points: *First*, the percentage of revenue spent upon the Army was very high when considered in comparison with this percentage in the case of other countries, (given at that time as, India 35 per cent, Russia 21 per cent, France 19 per cent, Japan 16 per cent, Italy 13 per cent). *Second*, the proportion of British troops to Indian in India (one to two) entailed an unnecessary burden upon the Indian tax-payer. *Third*, the army had been increased by 30,000 beyond the military needs of the country as laid down by the Army Commission of 1879, even though this Commission had taken into consideration the possibility of extensive operations with States lying beyond the North-West frontier of India. *Fourth*, the Indian Army was kept practically on a war footing, and thus was enormously expensive. Most of the countries of the West had adopted short-service systems, which enabled them to have large numbers of trained men available at short notice, whilst keeping down the numbers and expense of their permanent military establishments. This system had been adopted by England herself a quarter of a century before; but its benefits had not been extended to India. *Fifth*, there had taken place a great increase in the numbers of officers employed in the Indian Army; but at the same time the field of employment for Indian officers had been contracted rather than extended.

Throughout his life Gokhale kept up this campaign against the excessive military expenditure incurred by the Government of India, and against its unwillingness to provide facilities for Indians to take up a career as officers in the army. His position was thus summed up by himself:

'No pouring out of money like water on mere standing battalions can ever give India the military strength and preparedness which other civilised countries possess while the whole population is disarmed and the process of demilitarisation continues apace. . . . India is about the only country in the civilised world where the people are debarred from the privileges of citizen soldiership and from all voluntary participation in the responsibilities of national defence. . . . What I am anxious to see is the adoption of some plan whereby, while a position of greater self-respect is assigned to us in the work of national defence, the establishments necessary during peace and war times may be separated, and thus our finances may be freed from the intolerable pressure of an excessive and ever-growing military expenditure.'

Gokhale's position as a life-long leader of opposition meant that, with regard to great issues on which he was permanently convinced of the wrongness of the policy adopted by the Government of India—as for instance in this matter of military expenditure—he must continually, year after year, give voice to the same protests in a manner that should be both forcible and new. In this difficult task he succeeded to a very remarkable degree. He took infinite pains in adding new arguments and figures to the presentation of his case and in finding new angles and points of view from which to present it. His attitude was fearlessly critical of what he believed to be a great injustice to his country; but he managed to express his convictions in a manner which was moderate in tone and constructive in spirit, and he always succeeded in stimulating attention and interest, even in regard to questions at which he had been hammering for many years. In this matter of Army expenditure his main thesis continued the same—that the crushing weight of the military budget should be reduced by bringing into existence some system of Reserves, through which it should no longer be needful to keep the Army permanently on what approximated to a war-footing; that public defence should be made a matter of national concern by making it possible for members of the educated classes of India to take up the career of army officers; and that England should bear a part of the heavy cost of the Indian Army, since that Army was largely employed for purposes which ought to be regarded as imperial rather than Indian.

Indianisation of the Services

In his evidence before the Welby Commission, Gokhale laid emphasis upon another serious defect in the financial administration of his country, namely, the costliness of the great Indian Services. This also remained a matter upon which he continued till the end of his life to urge reform. Connected with this was the fact, upon which he laid great emphasis, that the proportion of Indians in the higher services was extremely small.

'The financial loss entailed by this practical monopoly by Europeans of the higher branches of the Services in India is not represented by salaries only. There are, besides, heavy pension and furlough charges, more than 3½ million sterling being paid to Europeans in England for the purpose in 1890. The excessive costliness of the foreign agency is not, however, its only evil. There is a moral evil which, if anything, is even greater. A kind of dwarfing or stunting of the Indian race is going on under the present system. We must live all the days of our life in an atmosphere of inferiority, and the tallest of us must bend, in order that the exigencies of the existing system may be satisfied. The upward impulse, if I may use such an expression, which every schoolboy at Eton or Harrow may feel, that he may one day be a Gladstone, a Nelson, or a Wellington, and which may draw forth all the best efforts of which he is capable, is denied to us. The full height to which our manhood is capable of rising can never be reached by us under the present system. The moral elevation which every self-governing people feels cannot be felt by us. Our administrative and military talents must gradually disappear, owing to sheer disuse, till at last our lot, as hewers of wood and drawers of water in our own country, is stereotyped.'

Gokhale proceeded then to show in the case of each of the Services how extremely small a share Indians had been given in the control of their country. It may seem of little advantage to recall such an incident in the story of a long fight which has now been largely won; but it must be remembered that here was an Indian who was unmistakably a born statesman bringing forward a thesis which was then almost new, at any rate in the august environment of a Royal Commission. In his fearless, but at the same time sane and reasonable statement of the Indian point of view regarding the Army, the Services, and other kindred subjects, Gokhale was striking the first great blow in a crusade which was to absorb his magnificent energies to the day of his death. The fact that, in this direction and that, the crusade has now been successful must lend the greater interest to this first major engagement.

EDUCATION

In regard to Education, Gokhale also expressed to the Welby Commission a point of view which was to become characteristic of him in the future.

'The meagreness of the Government assistance to public education in India is one of the gravest blots on the administration of Indian expenditure. No words can be too strong in condemning this neglect of what was solemnly accepted by the Court of Directors in 1854 as a sacred duty.

'There are more than 537 thousand towns and villages in India, with a total population of about 230 millions, and yet there are less than a 100 thousand public primary schools for them. The population of school-going age in India is about 35 millions, out of whom only about four millions, including those attending private or unaided schools, are under instruction, which means that out of every 100 children of school-going age 88 are growing up in darkness and ignorance, and consequent moral helplessness. Comment on these figures is really superfluous.'

The General Position of India

Such was the fashion in which Gokhale began his career as the spokesman of his country's aspirations and resentments before her English rulers. He summed matters up as regards the general position of India in the following terms:

'*First.*—The buffer of the Company's Government, which fairly protected Indian interests, is gone, and there is no effectual substitute.

'*Second.*—We have no effectual constitutional safeguards against the misapplication of our revenues for extra-Indian requirements.

'*Third.*—The control vested in the Council of the Secretary of State under the Statute of 1858, is rendered almost nugatory by the alteration of its status under recent Amending Acts.

'*Fourth.*—The control of Parliament, as against the Secretary of State, has become entirely nominal, owing to the latter being a member of the Imperial Executive, with a standing majority behind him. The old periodical inquiry by Parliament and its jealous watchfulness are gone. In fact we have at present all the disadvantages of Parliamentary Government without its advantages. In the case of all departments except the Indian, ex-ministers think it their duty, and also feel it to be their interest, to exercise the closest watch on the proceedings of their successors, with a view to passing the most adverse criticism that may be possible. In regard to India alone, ex-ministers vie with, and sometimes even go beyond, their successors in extolling all that exists and all that is done. The responsible opposition in this country thus abdicates its functions in the case of India only.

'*Fifth.*—The Government of India, as at present constituted, cannot be much interested in economy. Almost all internal administration having been made over to Local Governments under the Decentralisation Scheme, questions of foreign policy, large public works, and military questions absorb almost the whole attention of the Government of India. Further, the Finance Minister excepted, every other member of Council, including, since 1885, the Viceroy, has a direct interest in the increase of expenditure.

'*Sixth.*—Neither in England nor in India is there the salutary check of public opinion on the financial administration. Parliament is ill-informed and even indifferent. And the supreme and local Legislative Councils are simply powerless to control expenditure, since the Budgets have not to be passed, and no resolutions in reference to them can be moved.'

REMEDIES

To these defects in the existing condition of things Gokhale proposed the following remedies:

'*First.*—That the budget should be voted in the Supreme Legislative Council, in which an official majority should be retained.

'*Second.*—That a committee of control should be set up (in England), to which non-official members of the Supreme Council might have the right of appeal; the duty of reporting to Parliament from time to time on matters of Indian finance should be assigned to this committee; it should take cognizance of all appeals addressed to it as above, and should exercise general control over the administration of Indian expenditure.

'*Third.*—That Section 55 of the Act of 1858 should be amended. This section, as it stands at present, enacts that "except for preventing or repelling actual invasions of Her Majesty's Indian possessions, or under other sudden and urgent necessity, the revenues of India shall not, without the consent of both Houses of Parliament, be applicable to defray the expenses of any military operation carried on beyond the external possessions of such frontiers by Her Majesty's forces charged upon such revenues."

'He urged that this section should be so amended as to provide that, "except in cases of actual or threatened invasion, the revenues of India shall not be used for military operations beyond the natural frontiers of India (these frontiers being once for all defined), unless, at any rate, a part of such expenditure is put on the English estimates."

'*Fourth*.—That the Legislative Councils of Madras, Bombay, Bengal, the North West Provinces (i.e. the United Provinces), the Punjab and Burma should return one member each to the Imperial Parliament. "Six men in a House of 670 would introduce no disturbing factor, while the House will be in a position to ascertain Indian public opinion on the various questions coming up before it in a constitutional manner." He pointed out that the small French and Portuguese settlements in India already enjoyed a similar privilege.

'*Fifth*.—That special knowledge of finance be regarded as a necessary qualification of the Viceroy. "It would be a great advantage if the Viceroy, instead of being his own Minister for Foreign Affairs, were to be his own Finance Minister. At any rate the immediate connection with the Foreign Department should cease, the department being placed like other departments in charge of a separate member of the Executive Council."'

A study of Gokhale's evidence before the Welby Commission will show a very remarkable power of analysis and criticism with regard to the existing system of affairs. His concrete proposals, which have just been considered, give ample evidence of the powers which were developing in him, and which were to bear such ample fruit later in his life.

The Welby Commission, and After

Life in England

The experience of life in England was one of considerable strangeness from many points of view to the young Brahmin, who was orthodox in regard to the food he ate and the clothes he wore. One of his fellow-witnesses before the Commission,[1] who was brought into very close contact with him at the time, speaks thus of him:

'He was exceedingly shy. That shyness was greatly enhanced by reason of finding himself in strange company. To him it was wholly a new experience to live in an English house with English ladies and gentlemen and Parsees. He was a Hindu, and though on board the mail steamer he had seen something of cosmopolitan life and mixed with passengers of different races and creeds, he could not have realised till he had come to live with us what was domestic life in an English suburb.'

Moreover, on his way across France, Gokhale had the misfortune to suffer an accident, which had the effect of injuring his heart. His condition became serious; but on account of his shyness and strangeness he did not for some time let anyone know that anything was wrong. Finally, however, Mr. Wacha found out about his suffering, and a doctor was consulted, who took a very serious view of Gokhale's condition, declaring indeed that unless steps were promptly taken, death would result.

'Mrs. Congrave, a highly polished lady residing in that house, volunteered to work as Gokhale's nurse. No sister could have nursed better; and none could have kept Mr. Gokhale so cheerful and bright all through that serious illness.'

[1] Mr. D. E. Wacha.

Gopal Krishna Gokhale

Plague in India

During the time when he was absent in England on his work in connection with the Welby Commission, Gokhale's fellow-countrymen were becoming acquainted for the first time with that terrible scourge which has done so much damage in India ever since, bubonic plague. At first the nature of this disease and the right measures to adopt for combating it were very imperfectly understood; and when the plague reached Poona certain courses of action were initiated by the authorities which led to great popular discontent. Stringent regulations were put into force with regard to segregation, disinfection of houses, compulsory inspection of infected localities, and so forth. Moreover the very serious mistake was made of entrusting the enforcement of these new (and from the Indian point of view revolutionary and oppressive) measures to British troops, who, however well-meaning, could not be expected to understand popular prejudices and to deal with them in a tactful and sympathetic manner.

The consequence was that a loud outcry arose in Poona regarding the behaviour of the British soldiers, especially of those whose duties made it needful for them to intrude into the home-life of the people. A large number of correspondents from India, many of them gentlemen 'in a very respectable and responsible position in life, pleaders, professors and journalists,' began to write to Gokhale whilst he was still in England giving him lurid details of the horrors which were happening in the city which he loved so well, and accusing the Government of Bombay of gross mismanagement in having made arrangements under which such occurrences were possible. Gokhale unfortunately took the matter up without waiting for further proof of the reports which he had been receiving. As a result of the popular resentment in Poona two European officials had been shot on their way back from the Birthday celebrations at Government House. The news caused a great sensation in England, and certain English newspapers urged very drastic action in response to the murders. In an endeavour to counteract such proposals Gokhale made public use of the reports which he had received concerning the behaviour of the British troops which had led indirectly to the murders. The Government of Bombay took the matter up, and instituted an enquiry, which did not substantiate the accusation which Gokhale's friends had made. Thereupon Gokhale's agitation at home was stigmatised as malicious and false.

The Apology Incident

This was the atmosphere in which the young statesman, who had deserved so well of his country by his work before the Commission, returned to India. At Aden he was met by letters from some of the friends in Poona who had given him the false information, beseeching him not to reveal their identity to the Government. Gokhale had already decided to bear the whole responsibility for the affair. When he reached Poona he found himself unable to obtain the support of witnesses to the statements which he had made on his friends' authority in England. These friends, 'with the exception,' Mr. K. Natarajan tells us,[1] 'of Pandita Ramabai,' failed him in what he called 'his dark hour of trial.' Consequently he decided that the only honourable

[1] Natarajan, *G. K. Gokhale: The Man and His Message*, p. 2.

thing which he could do under the circumstances was to submit a full and unconditional apology to Government. In this decision Mr. Ranade and other friends upon whom he relied strongly supported him.

The apology created a tremendous sensation in India. It greatly increased the respect in which Gokhale was held by those whose respect was really worth having. In reputable and responsible quarters he came to be regarded as a man who put truth and honour above expediency or popularity; and who was therefore to be relied upon in the future. The moral courage which the apology had demanded was appreciated at its right worth.

On the other hand, however, the 'extremist' section of Indian opinion greeted the incident with a chorus of execration and insult. Gokhale was taunted with having betrayed the national cause, with having truckled to the foreign oppressor. His honourable straightforwardness was interpreted as despicable and time-serving cowardice. So fierce was the feeling aroused against him, in spite of his great services to the national cause in connection with the Welby Commission, that it appeared that his public career inevitably was at an end. There could be no future for one who had incurred, however honourably, such universal detestation amongst the rank and file of his fellow-countrymen.

Gokhale felt his position exceedingly keenly. His nature was a very sensitive one; and criticism, especially harsh and unjust criticism, always caused him great agony of mind. One of his friends has said of him:

> 'An adverse remark, casually made, was sufficient to upset his mind and to deprive him of sleep for the whole night.'

Yet he refused to give way before the storm which

had broken upon him. To one who reproached him, though in a friendly manner, on account of the ampleness of the apology, and the humiliation which (in the speaker's opinion) it had brought upon the country, he replied, with sorrow and dejection, but at the same time with a staunch determination:

'You can scarcely have an idea how sorry I feel to hear from you that my conduct has brought no little humiliation on my country. I accept that as your frank and honest opinion, and I take it for what it is worth. But I tell you that you will, I hope, live to see a day when I shall cover my country with glory by way of compensation for the wrong which I am alleged to have done to her; and then critics of your type, who are now running me to death, will be converted into my admirers.'[1]

As one of Gokhale's Indian biographers has observed:

'Thoughtful people will agree that under the circumstances he was fully justified both in giving the apology and in using the terms he did, and that the step he took was the noblest action of his life. Years hence, when the political questions of these days are forgotten or finally disposed of, this sacrifice of his position and prestige in the eyes of his countrymen, and his risking a complete voluntary eclipse as a public man, will be counted as his greatest title to the respect of posterity.'[2]

The Effect of the Apology Incident upon Gokhale

The incident had a decided effect upon Gokhale's character. On the one hand he became more than ever careless of popularity. He learnt to judge questions on their merits, and to take action accordingly, irrespective of what public opinion might or might not say. He

[1] Shahani, *op. cit.*, p. 97.

[2] Paranjpye, *op. cit.*, p. 40.

became more self-reliant, perhaps more reserved. On the other hand he learned to test his evidence more thoroughly before committing himself. He became more cautious and prudent.

'The apology incident raised him both with the Government and his own self. To the former his views thereafter were bound to be peculiarly deserving of consideration as proceeding from a man who understood his business and his honour no less. To his own self this incident imparted the strength to stand alone against the world, if only he had the support of his own convictions.'

One who knew Gokhale very well, and was in the closest touch with him for a number of years, has told the present writer that the meticulous sense of honour which Gokhale showed in this affair was characteristic of him in many different relationships. Both in public speeches and in the articles which he wrote for the press, he was always extremely careful to give credit to his opponents for the best possible intentions, and to represent their point of view, not in the worst light possible, but in the best. If in his personal relationships with other men he ever felt that he had acted wrongly, he would take especial pains afterwards to set things right. On one occasion he had been somewhat short-tempered with his private secretary, in connection with some business connected with the Press managed by the Servants of India Society. Very late that same night, when the person in question was asleep in his room, Gokhale came to his door and with unaffected humility asked his pardon for his rudeness to him earlier in the day.

The Welby Commission, and After

Plague Service

The 'apology incident,' as has already been observed, threatened for a time to put an end to Gokhale's public career. It was hard to see how any leader could survive vituperation so bitter as that which had been poured upon him for what was alleged to be the humiliation of his country. Gokhale was by no means crushed, however. The plague was still doing appalling damage in Poona; and there was urgent need for public-spirited service in connection with the sanitary measures which were needful in order to put a stop to the scourge. Accordingly he organised a band of volunteer workers, who went about in the infected areas of the city, doing all that they could to insure the enforcement of precautionary measures, and to help those who were already stricken with the disease. Gokhale himself worked at this exacting and dangerous task from morning to night, and was the means of bringing a great deal of effective help to his fellow-townsmen. His services were warmly acknowledged by the officials who were in charge of the campaign against plague.

Later, in view of the outcry which had been raised by the extremist party against inoculation as a means of combating plague, a Commission was appointed by Government to go into the question; and Gokhale was nominated as one of the members. A great deal of travelling was needful in connection with the work of this Commission, which brought in a report entirely favourable to inoculation; though Gokhale added a minute recommending greater care in the actual carrying out of the inoculation, which should be put into the hands of trained men. Unfortunately, however, the findings of the Commission did not allay the reactionary agitation which had been commenced against the best of all plague remedies.

This epoch in Gokhale's life was of importance as testifying to the disinterestedness of his public service. Here was a man who was not only a famous economist, a distinguished lecturer, and the acknowledged spokesman of his country's aspirations after constitutional advance, but a man whose patriotism was genuine enough to make him risk death by a horrible disease, in the effort to save his fellow-countrymen from that death.

In this way the memories of the apology incident gradually died away, and Gokhale came to be generally loved and trusted once more.

Gokhale's Attitude to the Problem of Unity

In later years, though his interests became more deeply engaged with national and imperial problems, Gokhale still continued to take the warmest interest in the well-being of the capital of Maharashtra. Many of his opponents were men whose Maratha patriotism was so intense as to blind them to the interest of India as a whole. But whilst Gokhale was a loyal Maratha, he showed an admirable wisdom and sanity in refusing to allow any sectional loyalty to interfere with his loyalty to India as a united nation. He could be enthusiastic for the well-being of Poona. He could serve, as he did for many years, as a member of her municipality, and as its president. He could risk his life to save her from plague. But this local patriotism was always rightly blended with a wider national patriotism.

The most significant illustration of this quality of balanced loyalty, by which the claims of sectional interest were given full weight, but were never permitted to interfere with national well-being, may be found in Gokhale's attitude to the perennial problem of Hindu-Moslem relationships. As has already been noticed, the extremist politicians, who were continually in bitter opposition to Gokhale, were the party of fanatical Maratha nationalism, and therefore the party of irreconcilable animosity against the Musalmans. From time immemorial Maratha nationalism had been built up on conflict against this secular enemy of the race; and in the present also the smouldering fires could easily be kindled into violent conflagration. It was true that the interests of India as a whole demanded, from every point of view, unity of outlook and effective co-operation between Hindus and Musalmans. But this consideration, which weighed so heavily with Gokhale, was beyond the restricted view of his opponents. Their slogan was, in effect, 'Maharashtra first; India if possible next; but the Musalmans nowhere.' Gokhale clearly preceived the fatal dangers of such a position, and stood like a rock for his principle of friendly co-operation with the Musalmans in the interests of India as a whole.

The effect of the two policies became evident at a later date. The spirit of extremism made it impossible, when constitutional reforms were introduced, to avoid the application of the fatal principle of communal electorates, which perpetuated the division of the country into two opposing camps. The animosity between the communities being what it was, the election of Hindu representatives to the legislatures by Hindus alone, and that of Musalman representatives by Musalmans alone, inevitably resulted in the choice of extreme Hindus on the one hand and of extreme Musalmans on the other; and thus the divisions became more and more pronounced. The Hindu-Muslim Pact arranged by the Congress of 1916 proved only a temporary palliative; for the roots of animosity remained deeply implanted in the two communities, and the elections for the reformed councils provided from time to time, through their consecration of the communal principle, a means of automatically keeping resentment alive. As soon as the temporary fervour of the non-co-operation movement subsided, discussion and riot broke out with increased bitterness; and the problem of inter-communal conflict remains to-day the most baffling and disheartening obstăcle in the pathway towards a free Indian nationhood.

Indeed the Pact of 1916 ultimately resulted in an aggravation of the prevailing animosity; for it introduced the principle of communal representation into the very heart of the national movement, and it bestowed upon the Musalmans an inequitable over-representation which was bound ultimately to lead to resentment and increased friction.

Gokhale looked at the whole question from the point of view of a statesman and a constitutionalist. He saw no hope in a policy of separate electorates, which would merely perpetuate divisions, and would give every opportunity for their becoming more bitter. He believed that it was essential for the future well-being of India that there should be joint electorates. At the same time he perceived that communal cleavage being what it was (and still is), separate representation must somehow be secured for the Musalmans; for otherwise their co-operation could never be gained in the coming democratic regime. He believed therefore that seats would have to be reserved for them in the legislatures of the future.

How was this to be done without introducing the principle of communal electorates?

Gokhale's final solution to this problem may be roughly sketched as follows:[1] There should be large constituencies, each returning several members, of whom one or more (according to the numerical proportions of the two communities in the area in question) must be Musalmans. But the electorates must not be divided. The Hindus should vote for the Musalman representative or representatives, and the Musalmans for the Hindu. In the case, for instance, of a constituency returning three members, of whom one was to be a Musalman, each Hindu would have three votes, one of which must be given to a Musalman candidate: and so also with the Musalman voters.

A system of communal representation secures, in practice, that the most anti-Hindu Musalmans and the most anti-Musalman Hindus will be elected; but under the system just outlined the most pro-Hindu Musalmans and the most pro-Musalman Hindus would be chosen. Thus the communal animosity, which has become so markedly embittered in recent years, would be decreased, instead of strengthened, by the introduction of democratic institutions.

There can be no question that Gokhale was right with regard to this contention. It is becoming every day more evident that communal hatred is the most serious of all obstacles to the development of a free Indian nationhood. It is the tragedy of the past twenty years of political evolution that Gokhale's advice regarding this supremely

[1] I am indebted for this outline of Gokhale's final position regarding Unity to a gentleman who was for many years in close touch with Gokhale.

important issue has not been followed, and that the building up of representative organs of government has been permitted to proceed along the lines of communal cleavage. The setting right of this tragic mistake will be the most important task of those responsible for future constitutional advance in India.

IV

WORK IN THE BOMBAY LEGISLATIVE COUNCIL

Famine Problems

GOKHALE'S work as a legislator begins from the early months of 1899, when he was elected as representative of the Municipalities of the Central Division of the Bombay Presidency to the Bombay Legislative Council. He remained a member of this body for some two years, during which his ability made a marked impression in Western India. These years were a period of famine, and of consequent financial depression; and Gokhale made many suggestions in the Legislative Council with regard to methods by which the famine administration of Government might be improved, and the difficulties consequent upon famine in the general work of Government overcome. He had himself had experience of village life, and he regarded himself as custodian of the rights of the peasants, and as champion of their cause in the terrible trials through which they were passing. He criticised the existing system of relief, on the ground that labour was too greatly concentrated on large relief works. Such large works give a great opportunity for the outbreak of epidemic diseases. They also require that the destitute people shall travel over large distances in order to reach the centre of relief; and amongst the ignorant and unprogressive classes who suffer first from a famine, the consequent home-sickness, leading to frequent absence from work, is a serious obstacle to the effectiveness of the relief. He also maintained that the Famine Code, for all its wisdom and beneficence, was too rigidly administered. There was a tendency to exact compliance with standards of work which were often beyond the capacity of the enfeebled workers; and, if the standards were not complied with, petty officials were apt to resort to fining, and to other disciplinary measures, which seriously interfered with the popularity and effectiveness of the relief given. He also maintained that the Bombay Government had been too niggardly with regard to the giving of gratuitous relief, and in this respect had lagged seriously behind other provincial Governments.

Gokhale never ceased to take a deep interest in famine-relief; and to the end of his life he continued the champion of the voiceless multitudes who are the chief sufferers from famines. Except perhaps with regard to his plea for enhanced liberality in the bestowing of gratuitous relief, in respect to which the evils of pauperisation are now felt to be more serious than he recognised, his main contentions have become axioms of famine-policy. Relief-works should be small and scattered, rather than large and concentrated. They should be so placed as to enable as large a proportion of workers as possible to return to their own homes every evening. There should be a wise measure of elasticity and leniency in regard to the exacting of given standards of work; and harsh disciplining of the workers should be sedulously avoided, as liable to lead to desertions and consequently to enhanced destitution.

Furthermore the spirit in which famine is now fought—a spirit which makes the organization and carrying through of a great famine-campaign in India one of the most beneficent activities ever engaged in by any government—may in no small degree be traced to Gokhale's persistent advocacy of the principle that the fearful tragedy of a famine should be regarded and dealt with as a great human problem, rather than as a matter merely of administrative machinery and technique.[1] Here, as in many other relations, Gokhale's strong sense of human values made his work for his country a genuine labour of love.

The Land Alienation Bill

Closely connected with the question of famine in the mind of Gokhale was the question of the land-revenue. Here again a highly complicated and technical economic problem became for him a matter of intense human interest; for he knew from his own experience what is meant in a village home by such stark facts as agricultural indebtedness and the incidence of the land-tax. During the time when he was a member of the Bombay Legislative Council a Land Alienation Bill was brought by Government before that Council. The purpose of the Bill was thoroughly sound—to provide the beginnings of a solution for the very serious problem constituted by the hopeless indebtedness of a large proportion of the peasantry who had fallen completely under the power of the village money-lenders. It was believed by Government that one of the chief reasons for this indebtedness was the power possessed

[1] The author of this book had occasion to see the working of these principles in actual practice during a period of service as a Famine Charge Officer in 1921.

by the peasants to mortgage their lands—often on exceedingly unfavourable terms. The result of their possession of this power was that the land was rapidly passing out of the hands of the peasants into those of the money-lenders, and that the peasants were tending to become mere tenants on an extremely insecure tenure of the lands which had been their ancestors' and their own. In a great number of cases, indeed, the position of the peasants was worse even than this; for their indebtedness was so great that they had fallen into the position of land-serfs, working upon fields which had been their own, for a miserable allowance of food, barely sufficient to keep body and soul together, this being all that the money-lenders, who took all the rest of the produce of the land in payment of their debts, would allow to them.

Government proposed to render this miserable subjection of the peasantry impossible, by restricting the power of the owner of land to mortgage his land and by allowing him to borrow only on the security of the year's crop. All lands which had been forfeited to Government on account of the inability of the holder to pay his land tax, and all waste lands in future to be brought under cultivation, whether through the progress of irrigation or in other ways, were to be granted by Government on a new kind of inalienable tenure, which, it was believed, would greatly strengthen the position of the peasantry against the money-lender.

The problems which the Land Alienation Bill were intended to solve had become more than usually pressing, owing to a succession of famine years; and the position of the peasants in Western India was indubitably very bad. Furthermore, anyone opposing the Bill laid himself open at once to the odious suggestion that he was an agent of the money-lenders, endeavouring to secure them in a position from which they were able to enslave the peasantry. The Government case was made out with great force and ability. The member of the Bombay Government who introduced the Bill in the Council had argued powerfully for the Government view that it was the existing fixity of tenure, and the power of transfer, which had reduced large numbers of the land-owning peasantry to the position first of rack-rented tenants and then almost to that of serfs. The Survey and Settlement Commissioner, with a wide-reaching knowledge of the conditions under which the peasants were living, and a genuine desire to improve their lot, had expressed his emphatic opinion that the only way of doing so was to restrict their powers of alienating their land.

None the less there was great public indignation against the Bill. A large number of petitions protesting that it was grossly unjust to the peasantry were sent in from political bodies such as the Bombay Presidency Association, the Sarvajanik Sabha and the Deccan Sabha. Meetings were held in the rural districts all over the Presidency and resolutions against the Bill were passed and forwarded to Government.

Gokhale's Opposition to the Bill

In this agitation Gokhale took a very prominent part. He realised as thoroughly as anyone the miserable condition of the peasants under existing circumstances. But he maintained that to seek to improve that condition by lessening the peasants' rights over their ancestral fields was not only morally unjustifiable, but was a gross betrayal of their true interests. The problem of agricultural indebtedness could only be solved by genuinely constructive statesmanship. The peasants must not be deprived of their rights in this way, but must be set in a position which would make it possible for them to stand on their own feet and to defend their rights for themselves, because they were economically independent. The effect of the proposed Bill would indeed be a disastrous weakening of the peasantry, instead of a strengthening, since it would enable the Government to confiscate land on account of non-payment of revenue for only one year. There would thus come about a wholesale process of nationalisation of the land, under which Government would be able to become the proprietor for a small fraction of the market value of the land.

His Speech

Some passages from Gokhale's speech delivered on August 23, 1901, at a meeting of the Bombay Legislative Council, Poona, will serve to indicate the grounds upon which he based his opposition to the Bill:

'The only party whose position is improved by the Bill are the Government themselves. I do not mean to say that the framers of the Bill have this object in view. But that cannot alter the fact that this will be the result of the proposed legislation. In the first place . . . the Bill constitutes an emphatic assertion of the principle of State-landlordism, and this is bound to have far-reaching consequences. The Bill means a nationalisation of forfeited lands, which alters completely the character of the land-tenure in the Presidency. . . .

'The wide discretionary powers which Government proposes to take under the Bill will enable them whenever they like—though this is not desired at present—to grant short leases or take land for public purposes without any compensation, or allot it to whomsoever they please. This is a real danger, because the tendency of revenue officers generally is to put the widest possible interpretation on the powers of Government, for the purpose of enhancing the Government revenue in every possible way.

'Does anyone imagine that a measure of such far-reaching tendencies would have been introduced in England and rushed through Parliament with so much precipitation in spite of the unanimous protests of the people? And I submit that the deliberation which becomes in England a duty of Government, owing to the power of the electors, should also be recognised by the British Government in India as a duty under a sense of self-restraint. What is the position here to-day? We, the elected members of this Council, are absolutely unanimous in resisting this Bill, and though our voting power is not large enough under the constitution of this Council to prevent the passing of any measure which Government are determined to carry, we represent, when we are unanimous, a moral force which it is not wise to ignore. For better or worse you have introduced the elective element into your Councils, and according to your own English ideas, you must now accept us as speaking not for ourselves individually, but in the name of those who have sent us here. And if a standing majority has been secured to Government under the Constitution, its real purpose, I take it, is not to enable Government to ride roughshod over our unanimous expression of opinion, but to prevent the non-official members from combining and overthrowing anything that Government may have done. This, I submit is the only true interpretation of the present constitution of this Council. . . .

'Nothing can fill us with greater sadness than this spectacle of Government trying to carry a measure in such haste and without proper deliberation—a measure that is bitterly resented by the agriculturalists, that has roused the apprehensions of the money-lenders, and that is condemned by the educated classes with one voice and in no uncertain terms. Is it fair, is it wise that Government should reduce us, the elected members, to a position of such utter helplessness that our united appeal should not secure even a brief postponement for a measure of such great importance?'

Gopal Krishna Gokhale

His Rebuttal of the Accusation of Supporting the Money-lenders'

The same speech delivered by Gokhale on this occasion, against the Land Alienation Bill of the Bombay Government, contained another notable passage, which throws light on the manner in which Gokhale felt himself called to be the defender of the common people, and shows how bitterly he had felt the accusation that his opposition to the Bill had been prompted merely by a narrow-minded and corrupt support of the money-lenders:

'I have with regret seen it suggested by some of the official supporters of the measure that the educated classes are not really in touch with, and do not understand, the true wishes and feelings of the great body of agriculturalists in this matter, and that their opinion on this Bill is not entitled to any weight. Such a suggestion, I submit with due deference, is inaccurate as a statement of fact and questionable in point of taste. How would these gentlemen like it, if we turned round and said, What do these Collectors and Assistant Collectors really understand of the true feelings of villagers? When they happen to go to a village, in the course of their official duties, what actually takes place is this: They pitch their tent at some distance from the place, unless there is a traveller's bungalow anywhere near, make a few enquiries of the village or *taluka* officials that are always in attendance, and visit, perhaps, a few spots in the neighbourhood. Their knowledge of the vernaculars no more qualifies them to enter into a free conversation with the villagers than does the English of Macaulay and Johnson, which we study, enable us to understand without difficulty the vigorous language of a British or Irish soldier. Meanwhile, it is the interest of the village officials that as few complaints should reach these officers as possible, and that they should go away well pleased; and the termination of the visit of inspection is regarded with feelings of genuine relief. I think such a way of putting the matter has in it just that amount of truth which makes the whole description look plausible. But I feel bound to say that it is grossly unfair to a large number of very deserving and very conscientious officers of Government. The truth is that the English officials in this country understand the ryot (the peasant) from one standpoint, and we understand him from another, and between the two our knowledge of him is certainly not the less deep or instinctive or accurate.

'Then again it has been stated that only the money-lenders and their champions are opposing this Bill, and to our great regret and astonishment we find the Secretary of State for India declaring in Parliament that it is all a money-lending agitation. Now all I can say in this matter is that there cannot be a more complete or a more grievous misapprehension of the true facts of the situation; and the circumstance that the Secretary of State should have lent the weight of his authority to this misapprehension shows to my mind how entirely out of touch those who are responsible for advising him are with the real sentiments of the agricultural population. The agitation against the Bill is emphatically not a money-lending agitation.

'We are not money-lenders ourselves, and there is no earthly reason why we should champion the interests of the money-lender more than those of the ryot, even if the instinctive sympathy which all human beings feel for the weaker party in any struggle were to be withheld by us from the poor ryot. And speaking for myself, . . . I will say this: that it was my privilege to receive my lessons in Indian Economics and Indian Finance at the feet of the late Mr. Justice Ranade, who was always a friend of the poor ryot, and who, it is well known, greatly interested himself in the passing and the subsequent successful administration of the Deccan Agriculturalists Relief Act. It is not therefore possible, unless I am prepared to play false to the teachings of my departed master, that in any agrarian discussion I should range myself against the interest of the ryot, or be swayed by a special feeling of partiality for the money-lender. No, my Lord, it is because I believe, and very firmly believe, that this Bill will prove disastrous to the best interest of the agriculturalists, and not because it is likely to do any harm to the money-lender—which I do not think it really will, that I deem it to be my duty to resist the passing of this measure to the utmost of my power. If it is true, as I have heard it alleged, that the agriculturalists themselves do not dislike this Bill, may I ask how it is that, while the petitions against the Bill have poured in upon the Council in a manner perfectly unprecedented—and many of them are signed by large numbers of agriculturalists—there is not a single petition from any agriculturalist in favour of the Bill.'

This extract demonstrates Gokhale's outstanding faculty of sane and moderate statement, and shows how ready he was to recognise the best in his opponents. He qualifies his assertion regarding the aloofness of the Government officials from the common people, by acknowledging that there were honourable exceptions. He repels the cruel suggestion, which had been made in the highest quarters, that the opposition to the Bill was support corruptly given to the money-lending interest, not with the passionate resentment which such a suggestion deserved, but with a courteous and restrained logic.

Constructive Suggestions

Gokhale's criticism of the Government proposals was not a merely negative one. He believed that the Bill constituted a measure of robbery directed at the most dearly-held privilege of the agriculturalist—namely, his unfettered rights over his land—but he knew that its motive was sound; for he had first-hand knowledge of the appalling evils of agricultural indebtedness. He fully realised that every effort must be made to free the ryot from the clutches of the money-lender; but he was convinced that a better method of achieving this end could be found than that of depriving the peasant of his rights over his own property. Consequently he suggested that the problem should be tackled by the starting of agricultural banks, from which the peasants would be able to obtain loans on easy terms, without the danger of falling into hopeless and permanent indebtedness:

> 'What the ryot needs is money, or what is nearly the same thing, cheap money. And if you do not reduce what he pays at present to the money-lender, or do not advance anything from the coffers of Government to help him, how can you give any relief to the ryot? It is, I submit, not possible to improve the position of the agriculturalist by a mere manipulation of the legislative machine.'

Thus began Gokhale's campaign for the improvement of the condition of the peasants by means of Co-operative Credit Societies, through which the existing burden of indebtedness might be taken over, the peasants freed from the money-lenders, and facilities be afforded for their obtaining cheap money when necessary for future needs. The position of the Indian agriculturalist was to be improved, not by a limitation of his rights but by a beneficent and constructive policy on the part of Government, which should relieve him of his burdens, and teach him through co-operative effort to avoid such burdens in the future, whilst placing within his reach that essential factor to his success—cheap money whereby he could tide over hard times.

The Land Alienation Bill was finally passed through the Bombay Legislative Council by the use of the official majority, and in face of the practically unanimous opposition of the elected members. As a protest against this procedure the elected members marched out of the Council Hall. The Act however was not largely applied, whilst the wide extension of co-operative credit societies, and their great success in the Bombay Presidency, has established the correctness of the point of view taken by Gokhale.

The District Municipal Act

Only one other considerable measure came before the Bombay Legislative Council during the time when Gokhale was a member of it. This was a Bill to amend the District Municipal Act, dealing with the constitution of municipalities, their functions, their conduct of business, the control of their accounts, and so forth. Gokhale was a member of the Poona Municipality for a number of years, and at a later period became President, in which capacity be did admirable work, introducing improved methods of business procedure into the municipal meetings, and in various ways making the work of the municipality more efficient and expeditious. He took great interest in the District Municipal Act, and was an active member of the Select Committee appointed in connection with it. The mover of the Bill referred appreciatively to his services in this connection. In one respect, however, Gokhale's apprehension was aroused by the Bill. He proposed an amendment to delete from it the words 'or by sections of the inhabitants' in regard to municipal elections; and he spoke as follows against any introduction of the principle of sectional representation into municipal politics:

'We value local self-government not only for the fact that local work thereby is better done, but also for the fact that it teaches men of different castes and creeds, who have long been kept more or less apart, to work together for a common purpose. There are, in all conscience, causes for differences enough among the different sections in this land, and I submit that the Legislature should not, in the best interest of the country, without the very strongest reasons, give any statutory recognition to these differences. There is nothing in the nature of local self-government which implies any conflict between the interests of one section and another.'

This utterance is notable as Gokhale's earliest enunciation as a legislator of the principle to which he afterwards attached so great importance, that the introduction of democratic institutions into India should be rigorously safeguarded from any tendency to sanction, or to accentuate, communal differences.

Temperance

Gokhale was also able to assist the cause of temperance during his time in the Bombay Legislative Council, by urging not only that Government should raise the price of intoxicants, but also that they should reduce the facilities for obtaining them. He believed on principle in total Prohibition, but until a policy of Prohibition became possible, he held that it was the duty of the authorities, in view of the ravages wrought by the drink-habit, especially amongst the poorer classes of the population, to make drink not only more expensive but also more hard to obtain.

The Spirit of His Work

Throughout this period of his life Gokhale was gaining invaluable inside experience of the problems of statesmanship. He was continuously engaged in the investigation of this aspect or that of the work of administration and legislation. He made very full use of the right of interpellation accorded to members of the Council; but he made his criticisms in a courteous and friendly spirit, which went far to secure adequate consideration by Government of the points which he raised. He proved many times over that he was not a destructive opponent of everything which Government might do, just because it was done by Government, but that his chief aim and desire was that the lot of his fellow-countrymen might be improved through the constructive co-operation of officials and non-officials in the cause of the people as a whole.

The Death of Mr. Ranade

In the midst of these activities, many of which entailed prolonged and painstaking research into various aspects of the administration, Gokhale suffered a great personal grief in the loss of his friend and guide, Mr. Justice Ranade. The relationship between these two men had been for some fifteen years a very close one; and the younger man felt that he owed his ideals and inspiration almost entirely to the elder, for whom he had a profound admiration and love. He wrote as follows to one of his own brilliant juniors concerning his loss:

'Since I wrote to you last, my great master, Mr. Ranade, has passed away. What his death means to me is more than I can tell you. I feel as though a sudden darkness has fallen upon my life, and the best part of the satisfaction of doing public work is, for the present at any rate, gone. Of course I recognise that it is my duty, as it is that of so many others, to struggle on, faintly it may be, but ever in faith and hope—trying in our own feeble manner to uphold the banner unfurled by him, cherishing with love and reverence the ideals to which he gave his matchless life. But it is a dreary task; and I do not know if men like myself will be enabled to accomplish even a small portion of it. However, the attempt must be made, and there happily the responsibility of us human beings ends.'

Work in the Bombay Legislative Council

One of the Indian biographers of Gokhale, himself a brilliant educationalist, writes thus of the relationship which had existed between Gokhale and Ranade, and which had borne such remarkable fruit in the training of the younger man for the service of his country:

'The story of this friendship is one of the most beautiful romances in modern Indian history. For years they were engaged together in the close study of the progress and destiny of nations, the inner meaning of public events, the far-off results of action, the discipline of failure, service and sacrifice, and the infinite play of human motive and passion, not only in profound treatises of political philosophy, but also in the ephemeral effusions of the daily press, and in ponderous government publications. Surely there is no fairer sight on earth than the close communion of two such kindred spirits, and it has brought untold blessings in its train on us all.'[1]

About the same time Gokhale lost his second wife. He did not marry again, his two daughters being entrusted to the care of some relatives for their upbringing.

Election to the Imperial Legislative Council

Early in 1902 ill-health led Mr. (afterwards Sir) Pherozeshah Mehta to resign his seat on the Imperial Legislative Council. This seat, which was filled by election from among the non-official members of the Bombay Legislative Council, was conferred upon Gokhale by a unanimous vote; and thus at the age of thirty-six he entered upon his career as the chief representative of his country in the central organ of Government. From that time till his death, a period of thirteen years, he worked incessantly in this capacity of imperial legislator at his task of expressing and rendering operative the

[1] J. B. Raju, *Gokhale*, p. 3.

view-point of enlightened Indian opinion. Under the constitutional arrangements then in existence much of his criticism of things as they were, and much also of his constructive suggestion for the future, had to be packed into the speeches delivered from year to year on the imperial Indian budget; and in consequence it will be found that a study of these speeches constitutes the best method of discovering what the mind of Gokhale really was regarding major national issues, and how he proposed to improve the existing condition of things in his country.

His Budget Speeches

These annual budget speeches came to be more and more important for the country as a whole; for the spirit in which they were delivered, and the constructive suggestions for the future with which they abounded, made them an invaluable indication of the way in which the Indian Government must move, if in a time of growing extremism it was to retain the goodwill and co-operation of the responsible sections of Indian opinion.

'Gokhale was to the last the most brilliant member of the Imperial Legislative Council, and was popularly called the Leader of the Indian Opposition, though he himself did not consider that his duty was merely to oppose Government, but that it was to put before Government the Indian point of view on every question. His annual budget speech was a treat to which everybody, both friend and opponent, looked forward, the one with delight, and the other with fear. An answer had to be given to his arguments, and it is not everybody who could do it at a moment's notice, if at all. On one occasion Lord Kitchener privately asked him the points on which he wished to touch so far as military expenditure was concerned; and out of consideration for the great soldier, who was no debater,

Gokhale did not emphasise certain points as much as he would have liked to. His budget speeches always bore their fruit in the succeeding years' budgets. He was always on the side of retrenchment, and did not want Government to take more from the tax-payers than was absolutely necessary.'[1]

This is the opinion of one who has since risen to high office as a legislator and administrator, concerning the significance of Gokhale's budget speeches.

Another well-known representative of responsible Indian opinion speaks as follows:

'Gokhale's entrance into the Viceroy's Council opens a new chapter of usefulness in his life, and some of his greatest triumphs were achieved there. His first budget speech delivered there, on the 26th March, 1902, came as a revelation to everyone in the country, official and non-official alike. Nothing like it has ever been known before in the history of Indian political life. Since then he has delivered twelve Budget speeches, and they have been looked forward to annually. As far back as 1904, during his very early years in the Viceroy's Council, Mr. Brodrick, then Secretary of State, wrote to the Governor-General in Council to give effect as far as possible to Mr. Gokhale's suggestions in forming the estimates for the following year; and the Budget of 1905–6 was in a real sense his triumph. Even the foremost of his political opponents, Lord Curzon, was led to say, "God has endowed him with extraordinary abilities, and he has freely placed them at the disposal of his country," and counted it a pleasure to cross swords with him as a foeman worthy of his steel. . . . Lord Minto, having heard the Budget speech of 1906, perhaps the greatest of all those great speeches, said that even in England there were very few men on the front benches capable of such an effort. Sir Edward Baker said that he could wish for nothing better than that Gokhale should succeed him as finance member. Sir Guy Fleetwood Wilson spoke of the Budget debates in the Viceroy's Council, in the absence of Mr. Gokhale, as the

[1] Paranjpye, *op. cit.*, p. 48.

play of *Hamlet* with Hamlet left out. Sir James Meston compared him to the great Gladstone in possessing the rare and happy knack of making facts and figures live and speak with a deep human voice. The Right Hon. E. S. Montagu, . . . writing about Mr. Gokhale says, "His grasp of things, both in essentials and in details, was not the least valuable of the assets that he brought to the service of his country. It is not too much to say that his annual contribution to the debate on the Budget proposals in India was one of the outstanding features of the proceedings of the Viceroy's Council, and was eagerly awaited, even by those who could not see eye to eye with him in his criticisms.'"[1]

These opinions are here quoted in order that, at the outset of a consideration of the work done by Gokhale as a member of the Central Legislature of India, it may be realised how profoundly that work impressed both his fellow-countrymen and English statesmen who came into contact with him. The fact that he was always in opposition, and therefore had no opportunity to put his principles into practical demonstration through actual legislation, may make his manifold activities during the next thirteen years appear unfruitful. As a matter of fact, however, those activities had a decisive effect upon the future of his country, not only through the financial reforms introduced as a result of his annual budget speeches, and not only through the influence which he exercised upon the constitutional changes connected with the names of Lord Minto and Lord Morley, but even more through the demonstration which they afforded, spread over so many years, of the fact that, given democratic conditions of government in India, a type of Indian statesman will emerge who is admirably equipped to utilise those institutions, in a spirit of con-

[1] Raju, *op. cit.*, p. 9.

structiveness and of moderation, for the well-being of his country.

Gokhale Leaves the Fergusson College

The new type of work which he was thus taking up, necessitating prolonged and frequent absences from Poona, made it no longer possible for Gokhale to continue his work as a professor in the Fergusson College. He had served for eighteen years in the Deccan Education Society, and during most of that time had undertaken, and successfully carried through, extremely onerous duties in connection with the raising of financial support for the society, most of his holidays being employed in this manner. His college lectures, especially during the latter part of his service, had been 'nothing short of weighty statements on all political, historical and economic questions'; and he had come to exercise a very remarkable influence upon his students.

The wrench which he felt on giving up this familiar form of life, and the doubts which assailed him on launching out into the career of a political leader, pure and simple, are finely expressed in the reply which he gave to a farewell address presented to him by the students of his college on 19 September, 1902. In reading this speech, it must be remembered that Gokhale was retiring from a post which brought him in the sure, if not princely, income of Rs. 75 p.m., and that in the future he and his family would have to depend upon a pension of Rs. 30 p.m. (about £25 per annum); and this after eighteen years of exhausting work, in the course of which many lakhs of rupees had passed through his hands. He was compelled, moreover, at the same time to relinquish the small additional income which he had been able to make as an examiner in the Bombay University.[1]

His Farewell Address to the College

He took the opportunity, when replying to the farewell address presented to him on retiring from the college, to review his past experience and to disclose a few of the hopes that drew him on to further service of his country.

Some of these revealing passages may fitly be reproduced here:

'I feel thankful, profoundly thankful, that it has pleased Providence to give it to me to discharge the solemn and onerous obligations of a vow taken so many years ago, under the influence of a youthful enthusiasm, and that, no matter what happens to me in the future, I shall always be able to look back with pleasure and pride on this part of my career, and say to myself, "Thank God, I was permitted to fulfil my pledge." But, side by side with this feeling of thankfulness there is a feeling of deep regret that my active work for this great institution is now at an end. . . . My decision has not been arrived at without a long and anxious examination of the whole position. In the first place, my health is not now what it once was. During the last term it was a matter of anxiety to me from week to week, and almost from day to day, how I should be able to finish my work without breaking down in the middle of the term. Even then, as many of you are aware, I was not able to perform my duties in the college with that strict regularity with which my colleagues were performing theirs; and one cannot help feeling that this is a

[1] Gokhale had become a Fellow of Bombay University in 1895, and for one year had also been a member of its Syndicate. Amongst many other activities in connection with the university, he had been largely responsible for the drafting of new courses in history and economics, and for the inclusion of political science in the B.A. course. He had also strongly advocated the retention of history as a compulsory subject in the B.A. course, as he was convinced of its usefulness as a means of training in citizenship.

very unsatisfactory position to be in, though never a word of complaint was heard from my colleagues. And I felt I had no right to put such a strain upon their indulgence.

'You know the golden rule that when you sit down to a repast, it is always well to rise a little hungry; and when you go to a friend's house, you should rather leave before your time than overstay his hospitality even by a day. I know my colleagues do not think that the illustrations apply. All the same, having worked for eighteen years, more or less under high pressure, I thought it was best for me to retire and leave the field to other workers.

'This, however, is not my sole reason for withdrawing from the college; and some of you are apt to think that it is not a very conclusive one either; and I will frankly tell you that another reason has influenced me in making up my mind, quite as much as this one. . . .

'I can only ask you to believe me when I say that it is purely from a sense of duty to the best interests of our country that I am seeking this position of greater freedom, but not necessarily of less responsibility. Public life in this country has few rewards and many trials and discouragements. The prospect of work to be done is vast, and no one can say what is on the other side—how all this work may end. But one thing is clear. Those who feel in the matter as I do must devote themselves to the work in a spirit of hope and faith, and seek only the satisfaction which comes of all disinterested exertions.

'This is not the place where I may speak of my future hopes or lines of work. But one thing I know, and it is this: Whether I am permitted to press onwards and prove of some little use to the public in another capacity, or whether I have to return a weather-beaten, tempest-tossed, ship-wrecked mariner, my thoughts, as you have said in your address, will constantly be with this institution; and on the other hand, I shall always be sure of a warm and hospitable welcome within these walls whenever I choose to come here.

'And now, before concluding, I wish to say one thing to the students of this college. . . .

'The principal moral interest of this institution is in the fact that it represents an idea and embodies an ideal. The idea is that Indians of the present day can bind themselves together, and putting aside all thoughts of worldly interests, work for a secular purpose with the zeal and enthusiasm which we generally find in the sphere of religion alone. The ideal is the ideal of self-help, that we may learn slowly but steadily to rely less and less upon others, however willing to bear our burdens, and more and more upon ourselves. I trust that you, the students of this college, will keep this character of this institution steadily before your eyes—that your devotion to it, your enthusiasm for it, will be commensurate with the nobility and importance of its work, that even when you feel disposed to criticise it, you will speak of it with that loving solicitude with which you mention a parent's fault, and that you will always do what lies in your power to further its interest and enlarge the sphere of its usefulness and influence.'

This farewell address to his old college is an excellent example of Gokhale's oratory. In it are combined the clarity and eloquence of expression, and the restrained expression of deep emotion, which are characteristic of all his best public speaking. The tone of loyal affection for his old college, which runs through the whole, gives us the man himself on the strongest and most typical side of his character—his capacity for losing himself in a great cause.

This same instrument of Gokhale's oratory was now to be employed with decisive effect in the counsels of the Central Government.

V

1902

WHEN Gokhale took his seat as member of the Imperial Council, and assumed, as his abilities inevitably required that he should, the rôle of leader of the Opposition, the Viceroy was Lord Curzon. From January, 1899, to November, 1905, his resolute will dominated the policy of the Government, and Gokhale found himself repeatedly constrained both to challenge the autocratic spirit of his rule and to oppose measures brought before the Council for its approval.

THE BUDGET SPEECH OF 1902

The financial policy adopted by Lord Curzon's Government had indeed, proved markedly successful by the year 1902. In spite of the disastrous famines which had occurred in the last few years, the Budget had not only been balanced, but a handsome surplus had been secured. When Gokhale entered the Imperial Legislative Council, he found a general state of satisfaction at this condition of affairs, and a tendency to congratulate Government, and especially the Finance Member, on the change from the constant deficits of recent years.

Gokhale found himself unable either to share in the general satisfaction or to join in the compliments. His first utterance in the Council was the first of his great Budget speeches, and it began as follows:

Gopal Krishna Gokhale

I fear I cannot conscientiously join in the congratulations which have been offered to the Hon. Finance Member on the huge surplus which the revised estimates show for last year. A surplus of seven crores of rupees[1] is perfectly unprecedented in the history of Indian finance, and coming as it does on the top of a series of similar surpluses realised when the country has been admittedly passing through very trying times, it illustrates to my mind in a painfully clear manner the utter absence of a due correspondence between the condition of the people and the condition of the finances of the country.

'Indeed, My Lord, the more I think about this matter the more I feel—and I trust Your Lordship will pardon me for speaking somewhat bluntly—that these surpluses constitute a double wrong to the community. They are a wrong in the first instance in that they exist at all—that Government should take so much more from the people than is needed in times of serious depression and suffering; and they are also a wrong, because they lend themselves to easy misinterpretation, and, among other things, render possible the phenomenal optimism of the Secretary of State for India, who seems to imagine that all is for the best in this best of lands.

Currency Surpluses

'A slight examination of these surpluses suffices to show that they are mainly, almost entirely, currency surpluses, resulting from the fact that Government still maintain the same high level of taxation which they considered to be necessary to secure financial equilibrium when the rupee stood at its lowest. The year when the rupee touched this lowest exchange value was 1894–5, the average rate of exchange realised in that year being only 13·1*d.* to the rupee. Government, however, had in the face of the falling rupee resolutely maintained an equilibrium between their revenue and expenditure by large and continuous additions to the taxation of the country, and thus even in the year 1894–5, when the rupee touched its lowest level, the national

[1] Seven crores of rupees = Rs. 70,000,000, or about £5,000,000.

account sheet showed a surplus of seventy lakhs of rupees.[1] From this point onwards, the currency legislation passed by Government in 1893 began to bear fruit, and the exchange value of the rupee began to rise steadily . . . In 1898–9 exchange established itself in the neighbourhood of 16*d.*—the average rate realised during the year being 15·98*d.*—and the year closed with a balance of 3·96 crores of rupees, after providing a crore for military operations on the frontier—thus inaugurating the era of substantial surpluses. Now we all know that a rise of 3*d.* in the exchange value of the rupee—from 13*d.* to 16*d.*—means a saving of between four and five crores of rupees to the Government of India on their Home Charges alone, and I think this fact is sufficient by itself to explain the huge surpluses of the last four or five years.

Taxation Increased in Spite of Famine

'Now I submit with all respect, that it is not a justifiable course to maintain taxation at the same high level when the rupee stands at 16*d.* that was thought to be necessary when it stood at 13*d.* During the last sixteen years, whenever deficits occurred, the Finance Member invariably attributed them to the falling rupee, and resorted to the expedient of additional taxation, explaining that that was the only way to avoid national bankruptcy. . . . The chief financial expedient employed to escape the embarrassment of the time was continuous additions to the taxation of the country. Nine years out of the first twelve after 1885 witnessed the imposition of new taxes. . . .

'The total additional revenue raised by these measures of taxation during the past sixteen years has been no less than 12·30 crores a year. But this is not all. The land-tax, too, has come in its own automatic way, for large augmentations during the period.

'Putting these two heads together, the total augmentation of public burdens during these years comes to over 15 crores. Such continuous piling up of tax on tax, and such ceaseless adding to the burdens of a suffering people, is probably

[1] Seventy lakhs of rupees=Rs. 7,000,000.

without precedent in the annals of finance. In India it was only during the first few years following the troubles of the Mutiny year that large additions were made to the taxation of the country; but the country was then on the flood-tide of a short-lived prosperity, and bore, though not without difficulty or complaint, the added burden. During the past 16 years the country has passed through a most severe phase of agricultural and industrial depression, and yet it has been called upon to accept these fresh burdens—year after year—increasing without interruption; and all this with a view to ensuring and maintaining a "strong financial position" proof against all assaults.

India Now Seriously Over-Taxed

'The broad result of this continued series of taxing measures has been *to fix the taxation of the country at a level far above the actual needs of the situation*; and it is the *fiscal status* so forced up and maintained, and not a normal expansion of revenue, that had enabled the financial administration during all these trying years not only to meet out of current revenues all sorts of charges, ordinary and extraordinary, but to present at the close of the period abounding surpluses, which the richest nation in Europe might well envy.

'*A taxation so forced* as not only to maintain a budgetary equilibrium but to yield as well "large, continuous, progressive surpluses" even in years of trial and suffering—is, I submit, against all accepted canons of finance. . . .

Delusion of Financial Prosperity

'But even thus—even after doing what the richest nations of Europe shrink from attempting, meeting all sorts of extraordinary charges, amounting to about 70 crores in sixteen years out of current revenues—we have "large, continuous, progressive surpluses," and this only shows that more money is being taken from the people than is right, necessary or advisable, or, in other words, the weight of public taxation has been fixed and maintained at an unjustifiably high level.

Taxation for financial equilibrium is what we all can understand; but taxation kept up in the face of all the difficulties and misfortunes of a period of excessive depression and for "large, continuous and progressive surpluses" is evidently a matter which requires justification. At all events, those who have followed the course of the financial history of this period will admit that the fact viewed *per se* that such "large, continuous and progressive surpluses" have occurred during the period—as a result not of a normal expansion of fiscal resources, but of a forced-up and heavy taxation—does not connote, as Lord George Hamilton[1] contends, an advancing material prosperity of the country, or argue any marvellous recuperative power on the part of the masses—as the Hon. Sir Edward Law urged last year. To them, at any rate, the apparent paradox of a suffering country and an overflowing treasury stands easily explained, and is a clear proof of the fact that the level of national taxation is kept unjustifiably high, even when Government are in a position to lower that level. . . .

THE SALT-DUTY

'As regards the reduction of the salt-duty, I do not think any words are needed from any one to establish the unquestioned hardship which the present rate imposes upon the poorest of the poor of our community. Government themselves have repeatedly admitted the hardship; but in these days, when we are all apt to have short memories, I think it will be useful to recall some of the utterances of men responsible for the Government of India in the matter. In 1888, when the duty was enhanced, Sir James Westland, the Finance Member, speaking on behalf of the Government of India, said: "It is with the greatest reluctance that Government finds itself obliged to have recourse to the salt-duty." Sir John Gorst, Under-Secretary of State for India, speaking a few days later in the House of Commons, referred to the matter in similar terms of regret. Lord Cross, then Secretary of State for India, in his Despatch to the Government of India, dated 12 April, 1888, wrote as follows:

[1] The then Secretary of State for India.

'"I do not . . . propose to comment at length on any of the measures adopted by your Government, except the general increase in duty on salt. While I do not dispute the conclusion of your Government that such an increase was under existing circumstances unavoidable, I am strongly of opinion that *it should be looked upon as temporary and that no effort should be spared to reduce the general duty as speedily as possible to the former rate.*"

'His Lordship further urged upon the attention of the Government of India the following weighty considerations on the point:

'"I will not dwell on the great regret with which I should at any time regard the imposition of additional burdens on the poorest classes of the population, through the taxation of a necessary of life; but apart from all general considerations of what is in such respects right and equitable, there are, as Your Excellency is well aware, in the case of the salt-duty in India weighty reasons for keeping it at as low a rate as possible. The policy enunciated by the Government in 1877 was to give to the people throughout India the means of obtaining an unlimited supply of salt at a very cheap rate; it being held that the interests of the people and of the public revenue were identical, and that the proper system was to levy a low duty on an unrestricted consumption. The success of that policy hitherto has been remarkable; while the duty has been greatly reduced, the consumption through this and other causes has largely increased. . . . The revenue is larger now than it was before the reforms commenced in 1877, and I see no reason to doubt that the consumption will continue to increase, if it be not checked by enhancement of the tax."

'Speaking again at a public meeting in England, Lord Cross took occasion to repeat his views that "he was convinced that *the earliest occasion should be taken to abrogate the increase in the salt-tax*" (28 February, 1889). In March of the same year Sir David Barbour, speaking in the Vice-regal Council with special reference to a proposal for the abolition of the Income Tax, observed:

'"I think it would be an injustice so gross as to amount to

a scandal if the Government were to take off the Income Tax while retaining the salt-duty at its present figure."

'In 1890 Sir John Gorst, in his speech on the Indian Budget in the House of Commons (14 August, 1890) remarked: "The tax (on salt) was no doubt a tax which ought to be removed and *would be removed as soon as it should be financially possible to do so.*"

'Similarly, Lord George Hamilton himself, in a speech on the Indian Budget Statement in the House of Commons (4 September, 1895) emphasised the necessity of reducing the salt-duty as early as possible, pointing out that no other tax pressed so heavily on the Indian people.

'In view of these repeated declarations it is a matter for great surprise, no less than for intense regret and disappointment, that Government have not taken the present opportunity to reduce a rate of duty, admittedly oppressive, on a prime necessary of life, which, as the late Professor Fawcett justly urged, should be "as free as the air we breathe and the water we drink."

'It may be noted that the consumption of salt during the last fourteen years has been almost stationary, not even keeping pace with the normal growth of the population—showing a rise of less than 6 per cent. in fourteen years against a rise of 18 per cent. in four years following the reduction of the duty in 1882—and that the average consumption of the article in India is admittedly less than is needed for purposes of healthful existence.

The Reduction of Army Expenditure

'It may be asked, How can the two things that I advocate simultaneously be achieved together, namely, a considerable reduction of taxation and a large increase in the outlay on education and other domestic reforms? My answer is that the only way to obtain both objects simultaneously is to reduce the overgrown military expenditure of the country. When the strength of the Army was increased in 1885 by troops in spite of the protest of the Finance and the Law Members of the Government of India, it was pointed out by those two officers that the then existing strength of the Army was really sufficient for all purposes of India—for keeping quiet within the borders and repelling aggression from abroad, and that if the contemplated increase was effected, it would only constitute a temptation to the Indian Government to undertake undesirable schemes of territorial aggrandizement. The Army Commission of 1879, after an exhaustive enquiry, had come to the same conclusion, viz. that the then strength of the Army was sufficient not merely for the work of maintaining internal peace, but also for repelling foreign aggression, even if Russia acted *with Afghanistan as an ally*. . . .

'What strength of the Army should be maintained in India is a question of high Imperial policy, in which we are not allowed a voice. But this, I think, we may claim, that if the strength maintained is in excess of India's own requirements, as it is now plainly proved to be, the cost of the excess portion should, as a mere matter of justice, be borne by the Imperial Government. Even on the narrower ground that the Army in India is required for the maintenance of British rule, England, I submit, is as much interested in the maintenance of this rule here as we are, and so it is only fair that a portion of the cost should be borne on the English estimates. If this were done, and if Indians were more widely employed in the public service of the country—more particularly in the special departments—Government will be able to reduce taxation, and yet find money for more education, better Provincial finance, active efforts for the industrial development of India after the manner of the Japanese Government, and various other schemes of internal reform. Then will Indian finance be really placed on a truly sound basis, and then will our public revenues be administered as those of a poor country like India should be administered.

Imperial Patriotism

'Your Lordship spoke the other day in terms of striking eloquence of the need there is of Indians now giving up narrow views or limited ideals, and feeling for the Empire with Englishmen that new complete patriotism which the situation demands. Now that is an aspiration which is dear to the heart of many of us also. But the fusion of interest between the two races will have to be much greater and the people of India allowed a more definite and a more intelligible place in the Empire before that aspiration is realised. . . . What is needed is that we should be enabled to feel that we have a Government national in spirit though foreign in *personnel*—a Government which subordinates all other considerations to the welfare of the Indian people, which resents the indignities offered to Indians abroad as though they were offered to Englishmen, and which endeavours by all means in its power to further the moral and material interests of the people in India and outside India.

'The statesman who evokes such a feeling among the Indian people will render a great and glorious service to this country, and will secure for himself an abiding place in the hearts of our people. Nay, he will do more—he will serve his own country in a true spirit of Imperialism—not the narrower Imperialism which regards the world as though it were made for one race only and looks upon subject races as if they were intended to be mere footstools of that race—but that nobler Imperialism which would enable all who are included in the Empire to share equally in its blessings and honours . . .'

This notable speech is worthy of close study on the part of any one who is interested in the development of Gokhale's personality and in the type of statesmanship which he represents. Although it was delivered very soon after he had first entered the Imperial Legislative Council, it will be found to contain a definite enunciation of the great principles to which he was destined to give the rest of his life. His untiring championship of the poverty-stricken and voiceless millions of the Indian common people; his indignation at a policy—and a policy unfortunately renewed in our own day—by which the poorest of the poor are made to pay a heavy impost on one of the prime necessities of life; his opposition to an extravagant expenditure upon the Army; his claim for Indianisation of the services; his appeal for a more generous treatment of the great 'nation-building' departments of expenditure, especially education; his intense interest in the position of Indians in the Empire as a whole—all these causes are already near to his heart, and are already championed with all the force of a mature political leadership. The speech shows, moreover, his admirable command of English; his restrained eloquence; his tactfulness, courtesy and urbanity, even in dealing with burning issues; his moderation and tolerance in denouncing what he felt to be gross injustice to the weak and defenceless; his capacity for laborious research in regard to statistics and to the previous history of the issues with which he dealt; his ability in marshalling with crushing weight arguments drawn from his opponents' own armoury; his use of quotation from authorities whom his opponents would at once accept, in order to maintain his own point of view; his vigorous and yet kindly power of sarcasm; and the enlightened imagination which enabled him to understand and to make just allowance for, not only the point of view of those who radically differed from himself, but the needs and distresses of those who suffered patiently, without any means of redress.

The speech also illustrates a certain fault which is to be found in Gokhale's public speaking, and which springs from the long years spent by him as a college professor. He is so eager to make his meaning clear to his hearers that he is apt occasionally to labour his points unduly, as a professional teacher is bound to labour his points in order to impart new knowledge to immature minds.

VI

1903

GOKHALE'S Budget speech of 1902 made a profound impression, not only upon his immediate hearers, but upon all India. It also had solid results. To his immense satisfaction the Salt Tax was gradually reduced by Government from Rs. 2–8–0 per maund to Re. 1–0–0 per maund: and thus a heavy burden was for the time being removed from the shoulders of the poorest classes of the Indian population. Increased grants were also made to education, sanitation and other causes whose claims Gokhale so tirelessly pressed; and Government was not slow to acknowledge the value of the constructive spirit shown by his criticisms as a whole.

The response which had thus been made to his appeals of the previous year was acknowledged by Gokhale in another notable speech, that on the Indian Budget of 1903, in the course of which he spoke as follows:

The Reduction of the Salt Tax

'I desire at the outset respectfully to associate myself with what has been said by my Hon. Colleagues, who have preceded me, in recognition of the important measures adopted by Government this year to give relief to the tax-payers of this country. . . .

'I sincerely rejoice that my Hon. Friend, the Finance Member, was at last able to advise Government that the time had come when the claims of the tax-payers, who have had to submit to continuous and ceaseless additions to the taxation of the country during the last eighteen years, to some measure of relief might be safely considered.

'As regards the particular form of relief decided upon by Government, I have nothing but the warmest congratulations to offer . . . and I respectfully beg leave to congratulate Government on the courage, the wisdom and the statesmanship of their decision. . . .

'I am surprised to hear the opinion expressed in some quarters that the reduction of the salt-duty will not really benefit the vast mass of our population, but that it will only mean larger profits to small traders and other middlemen. I think that those who express such an opinion not only ignore the usual effect on prices of competition among the sellers of commodities, but that they also ignore the very obvious lesson which the figures of salt consumption during the last twenty years teach us. . . .

'I am confident that what has happened before will happen again, and that the Finance Member will not have long to wait before he is able to announce that the consumption of salt is once again steadily on the increase, that the loss of revenue caused by the reduction in duty at present will be only a temporary loss, and that in a few years' time it will disappear altogether in consequence of increased consumption. . . .

'I trust it will be possible for Government to reduce this duty still further in the near future; for the consumption of salt, which in the time of Lord Lawrence was found to be about 12 lb. per head in some parts of India, is now not even 10 lb. per head, whereas the highest medical opinion lays down 20 lb. per head as a necessary standard for healthful existence.

The Excise Duty on Cotton Goods

'In the remarks which I made in the course of the Budget discussion of last year, I dwelt at some length on the heavy and continuous additions made by Government to the taxation of the country since 1886, and I urged that as the currency policy adopted by Government had put an end to their exchange difficulties, some relief should be given to the sorely-tried tax-payers by a reduction of the salt-duty, a raising of the taxable minimum limit of the income tax, and the abolition of the excise duty on cotton-goods. Two of these three prayers have been granted by Government this year, and it was much to be wished that they had seen their way to grant the third also. These excise-duties illustrate what John Stuart Mill has said about the Government of the people of one country by the people of another. They were levied not for revenue purposes but as a concession to the selfish agitation of Manchester. They are maintained owing to a disinclination on the part of Government to displease that same powerful interest, though the mill industry in this country, owing to various causes, not the least important of which is the currency policy of Government themselves, is in a state of fearful depression. . . . In no other country would such a phenomenon, of the Government taxing an internal industry—even when it was bordering on a state of collapse—for the benefit of a foreign competitor be possible, and I am inclined to believe that the Government of India themselves regret the retention of these duties as much as anyone else. I earnestly hope that, before another year is over, the Secretary of State for India and the British Cabinet will come to realise the great necessity and importance of abolishing these duties, whose continued maintenance is not only unjust to a great Indian industry, but also highly impolitic on account of the disastrous moral effect which it cannot fail to produce on the public mind of India.

Education

'I admit the exceptional character of our Government and the conflicting nature of the different interests which it has got to weigh before taking any decisive action in this matter. But after so many years of settled government and of unchallenged British supremacy, it is, I humbly submit, incumbent now upon the rulers of this country gradually to drop the exceptional character of this rule and to conform year by year more to those advanced notions of the functions of the State which have found such wide, I had almost said, such universal acceptance throughout the Western world. European States for years past have been like a number of huge military camps lying by the side of one another. And yet in the case of those countries, the necessity of military preparedness has not come, and does not come in the way of each Government doing its utmost in matters of popular education and of national industries and trade. Our record in this respect is so exceedingly meagre and unsatisfactory, even after making allowances for our peculiar situation, that it is almost painful to speak of it along with that of the Western nations. In Europe, America, Japan and Australia, the principle is now fully recognised that one of the most important duties of a Government is to promote the widest possible diffusion of education among its subjects. . . .

'It is obvious that an ignorant and illiterate nation can never make any solid progress, and must fall back in the race of life. What we therefore want—and want most urgently—is first of all a widespread diffusion of elementary education, an effective and comprehensive system of primary schools for the masses; and the longer the work is delayed, the more insuperable will be our difficulties in gaining for ourselves a recognized position among the nations of the world.

'The history of educational effort in this country during the last twenty years is sad and disheartening in the extreme. Lord Ripon's Government, which increased the State contribution to education by about 25 per cent., i.e. from 98 lakhs to 124 lakhs between 1880 and 1885, strongly recommended in passing orders upon the Report of the Education Commission of 1882, that local governments and administrations should make a substantial increase in their grants to Education, and promised special assistance to them from the revenues of the Government of India. But before the liberal policy thus recommended could be carried out, a situation was developed on the frontiers of India which led to increased military activity and the absorption of all available resources for army purposes, with the result that practically no additional funds were found for the work of education. And in 1888 the Government of India actually issued a resolution stating that as the duty of Government in regard to education was that of merely pioneering the way, and as that duty had on the whole been done, the contributions of the State to education should thereafter have a tendency to decrease.

'Thus while in the West the Governments of different countries were adopting one after another a system of compulsory and even free primary education for their subjects, in India alone the Government was anxious to see its paltry contribution to the education of the people steadily reduced! . . .

'Now that an era of substantial surpluses has set in, Government will not find themselves debarred from taking up the work in right earnest by financial difficulties. In this connection I respectfully desire to make one suggestion—viz. that henceforth, whenever there is a surplus, it should be appropriated to the work of promoting the educational and industrial interests of the country. At present these surpluses go to reduce the amount of our debt but, as the Hon. Sir Edward Law has pointed out in the financial statement, our burden of debt is by no means heavy, and there are valuable assets on the other side to cover the whole of it.

'Surpluses, after all, mean so much more taken from the people than is necessary for the purposes of the administration, and I think it is most unfair that these surplus revenues should be devoted to the reduction of a debt which is not at all excessive, when questions concerning the deepest welfare of the community and requiring to be taken in hand without any delay are put aside on the ground of want of funds. . . .

INDIANISATION

'There is one more question on which I beg leave to offer a few observations. The question of the wider employment of Indians in the higher branches of the Public Service of their own country is one which is intimately bound up, not only with the cause of economic administration, but also with the political elevation of the people of India. There is no other country in the world where young men of ability and education find themselves so completely shut out from all hope of ever participating in the higher responsibilities of office. Everywhere else the army and the navy offer careers to aspiring youths which draw forth from them the best efforts of which they are capable. These services, for us in this country, practically do not exist. The great Civil Service, which is entrusted with the task of general administration, is also very nearly a monopoly of Englishmen. But it is not of these that I propose to speak to-day. I recognise that, in the present position of India, our admission into these fields of high employment is bound to be very slow, and I can even understand the view that, for the purpose of maintaining British supremacy intact, there must be for many years to come a large preponderance of Englishmen in the ranks of these services. But, our exclusion from high office does not end here. In all the special departments, or Minor Services, as they are called, our position is even worse. . . .

A Policy of Drift

'What one regrets most in the present system of administration is that it favours so largely a policy of mere drift. The actual work of administration is principally in the hands of members of the Civil Service, who, taken as a body, are able and conscientious men; but none of them individually can command that prestige which is so essential for inaugurating any large scheme of policy involving a departure from the established order of things. The administrators on the other hand who come out direct from England, command, no doubt, the necessary prestige, but their term of office being limited to five years, they have not the opportunity, even if they had the will, to deal in an effective and thorough-going manner with the deeper problems of the administration. The result is that there is an inveterate tendency to keep things merely going, as though everyone said to himself "This will last *my* time."

'What the situation really demands is that a large and comprehensive scheme for the moral and material well-being of the people should be chalked out with patient care and foresight, and then it should be firmly and steadily adhered to, and the progress made examined almost from year to year. . . .'

Of none, perhaps, of all Gokhale's public utterances

can it be more justly said than of this great speech that the original must be read in full if the greatness of Gokhale's spirit is rightly to be understood. The effort to compress his thought into a bald and stilted summary is nowhere more lamentably sterile.

It must be realised, as we read what he said, that these are not mere words. They are concentrated political wisdom. They are statesmanship in action. They are the effective expression, not merely of a people's will, but of a first-class practical ability in the task of indicating the manner in which that will may be put into operation. That they are such is proved by the fact that already, after little more than a year in the Council, by the cogency of his arguments and the sanity and reasonableness of his attitude, Gokhale had carried through to success the first campaign in his long war against extravagance and excessive taxation. His advocacy of the cause of the poor had already secured the reduction of the salt tax. To have achieved this, and in so short a time, proved him at once to be a statesman head and shoulders above all his contemporaries in India.

About this time Mr. Gandhi came into close relationship with Gokhale and found him deeply sympathetic with his efforts on behalf of Indians in South Africa. This was a cause to which Gokhale was at a later period to render important service, but at this earlier period he won a place in the hearts of the younger men which Mr. Gandhi affirms to be 'absolutely unique.' He was most ready to place all the wisdom of his political experience at the disposal of one who was seeking to serve the cause of the Indian people as Mr. Gandhi was. The latter's first impression of admiration was fully confirmed when shortly afterwards he was the guest of Mr. Gokhale in Calcutta. He describes the activities of Mr. Gokhale in connection with his duties in the Imperial Council and the spirit in which he discharged them as follows:

'To see Gokhale at work was as much a joy as an education. He never wasted a minute. His private relations and friendships were all for public good. All his talks had reference only to the good of the country, and were absolutely free from any trace of untruth or insincerity. India's poverty and subjection were matters of constant and exclusive concern to him.'[1]

The Official Secrets Act

In the same year, 1903, Gokhale made a notable pronouncement on the subject of the freedom of speech and of the Press. The occasion was the introduction into the Imperial Council by Government of a new Official Secrets Act, in regard to which Gokhale spoke as follows:

'This Bill, both in its principle and its details, is open to such grave objection that it is a matter for profound regret that Government should ever have thought of introducing the measure. The *Englishman*,[2] in a recent issue, describes the Bill as calculated to Russianise the Indian administration, and says that "it is inconceivable that such an enactment can be placed on the statute-book even in India." This, no doubt, is strong language, but I think it is none too strong, and in view of the quarter from which it comes it should give Government pause. . . .

'The present Bill proposes to make alterations of so astounding a nature in the former Act that it is difficult to speak of them with that restraint which should characterise all utterances in this Chamber. To state the matter briefly,

[1] M. K. Gandhi, *The Story of My Experiments with Truth*, vol. I, p. 537.

[2] A Calcutta newspaper representing the point of view of the English community in India.

the Bill proposes to make three principal changes in the old Act: first, it proposes to place Civil matters on a level with Naval and Military matters; secondly, in place of the present provision that a person who enters an office for the purpose of wrongfully obtaining information is liable to be punished under the Act, it is now proposed to enact that whoever, "without lawful authority or permission (the proof whereof shall be upon him), goes to a Government office," commits an offence under the Act; and thirdly, it is proposed to make all offences under the Act cognizable and non-bailable. Now it is difficult to imagine that any responsible officer of Government conversant in any degree with the administration of the country, and possessing the least regard for the professed character of British rule, could have drafted these amendments. Take the first proposal, to place Civil matters on a level with Naval and Military matters. The Civil administration of the country ranges from the highest concerns of State policy which engage the attention of the Viceroy, down to the pettiest details of the routine work of a village official. The word "secret" is nowhere defined, and it must, therefore, include all official information not authoritatively notified by the Government to the public. And I want to know if it is seriously intended to make the publication of even the most trivial news in connection with this vast Civil administration of the country penal—such news, for instance, as the transfer of a Government officer from one place to another—unless it has first appeared in a Government resolution or any other official notification. And yet this would be the effect of the proposed amendment. . . .

'I think that in a country like India, while Naval and Military secrets ought to be protected, if anything, with even greater strictness than in England, the very reverse is the case with matters concerning the Civil administration. The responsibility of the Government to the people in this country is merely moral; it is not legal, as in the West. There is no machinery here, as in Western countries, to secure that the interests of the general public will not be sacrificed in favour of a class. The criticism of the Indian Press is the only outward check operating continuously upon the conduct of a bureaucracy possessing absolute and uncontrolled power. . . .

'As regards the second amendment, which would make a man's merely going to an office without lawful authority or permission an offence, I am sure Government have not considered what this will mean in practice. A very large amount of the work of lower officials is transacted by the people concerned going to their offices without permission expressly obtained. Petitioners, for instance, often have to go to offices for making inquiries about what has happened to their petitions. They rarely receive written replies, and it will now be in the power of any police officer to get a man against whom he has a grudge, or from whom he wants to extort anything, into trouble by alleging that he had gone to an office of Government "without lawful authority." This will be putting a most dangerous power into the hands of the lower police, about whose character, as a class, the less said the better. Even an innocent friendly visit by a private individual to an official friend of his at the latter's office can, under this Bill, be construed into an offence. I am sure nothing could be farther from the intention of Government, and I am astonished that greater care was not taken in drafting the Bill to confine it to the object Government had in view.

'Lastly, it is proposed to make offences under this Act cognizable and non-bailable—which means that a person charged with an offence under this Act is to be arrested at once, but he is not to be liberated on bail—and yet there is to be no trial till the sanction of the Local Government has been obtained. This may take weeks and even months, and finally it may never be accorded, and the person arrested is all the while to rot in detention. I cannot understand how a procedure so abhorrent to ordinary notions of fairness should have commended itself to Government.

'The only redeeming feature in this most deplorable business is that among the opinions which the Government of India have received from their own officers, there are some who strongly deprecate the measure—at least in its more serious aspects. And I think it is a matter for special satisfaction that the Government of Bengal has spoken out so plainly against placing Civil matters on a level with the Naval and Military.

'I protest against the very introduction of this Bill. I protest against the spirit in which it has been conceived. I protest against its provisions generally.'

Gokhale and Curzon

The 'Russianisation' of the Indian Administration which in the case of this measure had been pilloried by a leading European journal of Calcutta, and which Gokhale had attacked so vigorously in the speech just recorded, was unfortunately a characteristic of much of Lord Curzon's activity. That Viceroy had a magnificent store of energy, and a great regard for scientific efficiency in administration; but he was heavy-handed, unsympathetic, and no believer in freedom. In consequence his rule, especially in its later years, drove the intelligent sections of Indian opinion to a frenzy of exasperation.

At a later date Gokhale himself spoke as follows of Lord Curzon:

'In some respects His Lordship will always be recognised as one of the greatest Englishmen that ever came out to this country. His wonderful intellectual gifts, his brilliant powers of expression, his phenomenal energy, his boundless enthusiasm for work—these will ever be a theme of just and unstinted praise. But the gods are jealous, and amidst such lavish endowments they withheld from him a sympathetic imagination, without which no man can ever understand an alien people; and it is a sad truth that to the end of his administration Lord Curzon did not really understand the people of India. This was at the root of his many inconsistencies, and made him a perpetual puzzle to most men. . . . Taking Lord Curzon at his highest, we find him engaged in a Herculean attempt to strengthen the Englishman's monopoly of power in India and stem the tide of popular agitation and discontent, by rousing the members of the bureaucracy to a sense of duty similar to his own and raising the standard of administrative ability all round. The attempt has failed, as it was bound to fail. Never was discontent in India more acute and widespread than when the late Viceroy laid down the reins of office; and as regards the bureaucratic monopoly of power, I think we are sensibly nearer the time when it will be successfully assailed.'[1]

The Universities Bill

In 1903 also Gokhale made the following valuable observations in the course of a speech on Lord Curzon's reactionary Universities Bill:

'Let not Government imagine that unless the education imparted by colleges is the highest which is at the present day possible, it is likely to prove useless and even pernicious; and secondly, let not the achievements of our graduates in the intellectual field be accepted as the sole, or even the most important, test to determine the utility of this education. I think—and this is a matter of deep conviction with me—that, in the present circumstances of India, all Western education is valuable and useful. If it is the highest that under the circumstances is possible, so much the better. But even if it is not the highest, it must not on that account be rejected.

'I believe the life of a people—whether in the political or social or industrial or intellectual field—is an organic whole, and no striking progress in any particular field is to be looked for, unless there be room for the free movement of the energies of the people in all fields. To my mind the greatest work of Western education in the present state of India is not so much the encouragement of learning as the liberation of the Indian mind from the thraldom of old-world ideas, and the assimilation of all that is highest and best in the life and thought and character of the West.

'For this purpose not only the highest but *all* Western education is useful. I think Englishmen should have more faith in the influence of their history and their literature. And whenever they are inclined to feel annoyed at the

[1] Presidential address at Benares Congress, 1905.

utterances of a discontented B.A., let them realize that he is but an accident of the present period of transition in India, and that they should no more lose faith in the results of Western education on this account than should my countrymen question the ultimate aim of British rule in this land, because not every Englishman who comes out to India realizes the true character of England's mission here. . . .

'It is to my mind a painful and significant circumstance that the present condemnation of the educated classes has been passed at the instance of men engaged in the work of education. I am astonished that these men do not realise that a part at least of this condemnation is bound to recoil on their own heads. The Hon. Mr. Pedler has told the Council of dishonest clerks, unscrupulous managers of colleges, and convict graduates. I do hope, for the Hon. Member's own sake as much as for the credit of the educated classes, that there has been another and a brighter side to his experience. Else what a sad sense of failure he must carry with him in his retirement!

'Happily, all educationalists have not been so unfortunate in their experience, not, if I may say so, so one-sided in their judgments. There have been men among them who have regarded the affection and reverence of their pupils as their most valued possession, who have looked upon the educated classes with a feeling of pride, and who have always stood up for them whenever anyone has ventured to assail them. One such professor, within my experience, was Dr. Wordsworth, grandson of the great poet—a man honoured and beloved as few Englishmen have been on our side of India. Another such man is Mr. Selby, whose approaching retirement will inflict a most severe loss on the Education Department of our Presidency. I am aware that it is invidious to mention names; but these two men have exercised such abiding influence over successive generations of students during their time that I feel no hesitation in offering a special tribute of recognition and gratitude to them. Their hold over the minds of their pupils has been due, not only to their intellectual attainments, but also to their deep sympathy with them as a class which they had helped to create. I believe that such men have never had occasion to complain that their views on any subject did not receive at the hands of educated Indians the consideration that was due to them.

'It is through such men that some of England's best work in India is done. It is these men who present to the Indian mind the best side of English character and English culture. It is such men that are primarily wanted for the work of higher education in India in the present state of things, and the best interests of both the rulers and the ruled may safely be entrusted to their keeping. I think that there is practically no limit to the influence which a truly great professor, who adds to his intellectual attainments sympathy and love for his pupils, may exercise over the minds of Indian students, whose natural attitude towards a teacher, inherited through a long course of centuries, is one of profound reverence.

'The recent Resolution of the Government of India on the subject of Education strikes the right note when it says: "Where the problems to be solved are so complex, and the interests at stake so momentous, India is entitled to ask for the highest intellect and culture that either English or Indian seats of learning can furnish for her needs." If the principle enunciated in this sentence be faithfully acted upon, it will go a long way to counteract the evil which is apprehended from the passage of this Bill. How far, however, this will be done remains to be seen. Meanwhile the old order will change, yielding place to new. One cannot contemplate without deep emotion the disappearance of this old order; for with all its faults, it had obtained a strong hold on our attachment and our reverence, and round it had sprung up some of our most cherished aspirations. For the present, however, the hands of the clock have been put back; and though this by itself cannot stop the progress of the clock while the spring continues wound and the pendulum swings, there can be no doubt that the work done to-day in this Council Chamber will be regarded with sorrow all over the country for a long time to come.'

There is no better example than this speech of the remarkable faculty possessed by Gokhale for taking a defeat in a manner which ensured future success. He was an admirable 'loser.' Even on a subject concerning which he felt exceedingly deeply, as he felt with regard to this question of autonomy in the universities, he was able to give a plain expression of his real feelings in a spirit of urbanity and moderation which in itself went far to prepare the ground for the future reversal of the mistake which had been made. A distinguished Indian educationalist,[1] an Englishman who spent many years in high office under Government, administering the educational system in two great provinces—has in a recent work declared that the autonomy enjoyed under present conditions by the Indian universities is one of the most healthy and encouraging features of the whole field of Indian education. Gokhale knew that he was right in championing such autonomy. He knew that the stars in their courses fought for him. He realised also his own impotence—the fact that he was fated ever to contend against an official *bloc* which at a word from above would remorselessly vote him down, however right he might be. Under such circumstances many a statesman would have given up in despair, or would have become permanently cynical and embittered. Gokhale kept his friendly good-humour through it all; and the fact that he did so made it inevitable that at last the good sense of his opponents would respond to this spirit and ensure the ultimate victory of his cause.

The speech on the Indian Universities Bill is also one of Gokhale's best performances in regard to its mellow humour—the friendly manner in which he poked fun at the professorial experts, and at the jeremiads of the Hon. Mr. Pedler—and from the point of view of its insistence upon the necessity of sympathy and understanding for

[1] Arthur Mayhew, in *The Education of India*.

their pupils on the part of Indian educationalists. It contains also one of Gokhale's most striking appeals for the fuller participation of Indians in the administration of their own country; and a noble vindication of the necessity for freedom as the basis of relationships between England and India.

THE VALIDATION ACT

The University Act soon began to prove difficult to work; and a year later (in 1905) Government introduced a Validation Bill into the Imperial Council, which Gokhale strenuously opposed, in a speech which contains an important enunciation of constitutional principles:

'In all civilised countries there is a well-understood and well-defined distinction between the Legislature and the Executive Government, and the Legislature is regarded as higher than the Executive. In India unfortunately this distinction for the most part is of only a nominal character; for, with the present constitution of the Councils, the Executive Government can get what law they please passed by the Legislature without the slightest difficulty. I submit however that it is not desirable, it is not wise, that this fact should be forced on the attention of the public in so unpleasant a manner as on this occasion, and I think the distinction becomes a farce if our Legislature is thus to be at the beck and call of the Executive Government, and if it is to be called upon to exercise its powers of legislation to remedy defects, not in existing laws, but in executive action taken under those laws.

'I respectfully but emphatically protest against this lowering of the dignity of the Legislature. Of course there is nothing to prevent the Government legally from coming to the Legislature with such proposals as they please. But I venture to think that there are moral limits on the competency of the Government in this matter. I think that the Government should come forward with proposals of amendment only in the event of the existing law being found so defective as to be unworkable, errors in executive action being set right as far as possible by executive action alone. . . .

'I have no wish to-day to stir up the ashes of the controversy that raged round the Universities Bill last year, though one may say in passing that some of the fears then expressed by the opponents of the measure about the probable exclusion of independent Indians from the administration of the universities are already being more or less realised. What, for instance, can be more lamentable than that, on the present Syndicate of the Calcutta University, four Faculties out of five should be without a single Indian representative, and that in Bombay a man like Sir Pherozeshah Mehta—once a Dean in Arts, who in point of attainments and of zealous devotion to the best interests of the country towers head and shoulders above many of those who have of late being posing as authorities on higher education in this land—should be excluded from the Faculty of Arts! However I know that any further complaint in this Council about the policy of last year's Bill is like ploughing the sands of the seashore, and I have no wish to engage in an enterprise at once so fruitless and so unnecessary. . . .

'I have already spoken thrice on this Bill, but I cannot let it pass without a final word of protest. British rule in this country has hitherto been described—and, on the whole, with good reason—as the reign of law. A few more measures however like the present, and that description will have to be abandoned and another substituted for it, namely, the reign of Executive irresponsibility and validating legislation.

'The Government are paying too great a price for what is undoubtedly an attempt to save the prestige of its officers. But is prestige ever so saved? On the other hand, an occasional admission of fallibility is not bad, especially for a strong Government like the British Government. It introduces a touch of the human into what ordinarily moves with machine-like rigidity. It enhances the respect of the people for law, because they are enabled to realize that even the Government respects it. And it strengthens the hold of the Government on the people, because they see that, in spite of its strength, it has a tender and scrupulous regard for the limitations imposed by the Legislature upon it.

'My Lord, may I in this connection say one word about Your Lordship personally? Whatever differences of opinion there may be in the country about some of the measures of Your Lordship's administration, the impression hitherto has been general that during your time the local governments and administrations have had to realize more fully than before that there is a controlling and vigilant authority over them at the head, and that this authority will tolerate no irregularities on their part. It is a matter of disappointment that this impression should not have been justified in the present instance. Public opinion in this country being as feeble as it is, the only two bodies that control the exercise of absolute power by the Executive are the Legislature which lays down the law, and the High Courts which see that the law is obeyed. If now the Government is to destroy the protection which the High Courts afford by means of validating legislation, and if the Legislature is to be reduced to the position of a mere handmaid of the Executive, to be utilized for passing such legislation, what is there left to stand between the people and the irresponsible will of the Executive?

'I feel keenly this humiliation of my country's Legislature; for though we Indian members have at present a very minor and almost insignificant part in its deliberations, it is after all our country's Legislature. Moreover, I have faith that in the fulness of time our position in it will be much more satisfactory than at present, and anything that lowers it in the eyes of my countrymen cannot but be regarded with profound regret.'

Apart from the important constitutional principles which it enunciates, this speech is noteworthy for the gentle irony with which Gokhale spoke of the salutary effect of an 'occasional admission of fallibility,' and for the good humour and dignity with which he filled his position as the champion of a hopeless 'though to his mind supremely important' cause who was called upon to face impossible odds. As has been observed before, the fact that this cause, and other causes to which he devoted himself, have subsequently triumphed is largely to be accounted for by the spirit in which Gokhale himself took continual and monotonous defeat, never despairing, never becoming embittered, continually building for the future upon the scanty foundations which were all that the present offered to him.

VII

1905

The Budget Speech of 1905

THE Budget Speech of 1904 was not of outstanding importance. That of 1905 was a notable utterance. It contained passages which reveal Gokhale as still patient and courageous in his task of educating India's rulers:

'There is but one feeling throughout the country—and it is a feeling of deep and unalloyed satisfaction—as to the manner in which the Government of India have decided to apply about 3¾ crores of the excess of their revenue over expenditure to measures of remission of taxation, administrative improvement, and the general well-being of the people.

The Reduction of the Salt-duty

'I heartily welcome the further reduction of the salt-duty by eight annas a maund. The duty now stands, as the Hon. Member rightly claims, at a lower rate than it has ever done during the last quarter of a century. In urging this measure of relief last year, I ventured to observe—

'"The salt-duty was reduced by eight annas last year, and the measure of relief was received with deep gratitude throughout the country. The reduction might, however, be carried still further without any inconvenience. The salt-duty question in India is essentially a poor man's question for it is the poorer many—and not the richer few—who eat more salt when it is cheap, and less when it is dear. The soundest policy in the matter—even financially—would therefore seem to be to raise an expanding revenue on an expanding consumption under a diminishing scale of duties."

'The only reply which was then vouchsafed to my appeal by our late Finance Minister, Sir Edward Law, was the remark that I was "one of the multitude who stand at the door of the Treasury and always cry, Give, give!" I rejoice therefore to find that in less than a year Government have seen their way to effect this reduction, and I am confident that a rapid increase in consumption will follow, wiping out before long the loss that has been caused to the Exchequer, and demonstrating also the wisdom of the course adopted by Government. . . .

Grants to Various Purposes

'The grant of 35 lakhs to Provincial Governments for additional expenditure on Primary Education is also an important step in the right direction, the field of mass education being one in which what has already been done is but little, as has been admitted by the Government of India in their resolution of last year on the subject, compared with what remains to be done.

'The grant of 20 lakhs for agricultural research, experiment and instruction, and the announcement that the ultimate aim of Government in this matter is "the establishment of an experimental farm in each large tract of country of which the agricultural conditions are approximately homogeneous, to be supplemented by numerous demonstration farms, the creation of an agricultural college, teaching up to a three years' course in each of the larger provinces, and the provision of an expert staff in connection with these colleges for purposes of research as well as education," indicate that the Government have at last made up their mind to recognize in a practical manner the supreme importance of scientific agriculture in this land. Twenty lakhs a year for such a purpose for the whole of India is of course totally inadequate; but it is a good beginning, and the Government have undertaken to find steadily increasing funds till the whole programme is properly carried out.

'The last measure to which a part of the surplus is proposed to be devoted, is a grant-in-aid of the funds of District and Local Boards throughout India, amounting in all to about 56½ lakhs a year, and equal approximately to one-fourth of the income of these Boards. This, to my mind, is one of the most interesting features of this year's Budget, and it is a feature on which I offer my heartiest congratulations to the Hon. Member. It means a frank acknowledgment of the claims of Local Bodies to participate in the financial prosperity of the Government of India, and a recognition of the fact that without the aid of Government the resources of these bodies are utterly inadequate to the proper discharge of the various duties laid on them.

'The last National Congress, which met in Bombay, urged such assistance to Municipal and Local Boards; and I rejoice to find that Government have responded, at least partially, to the appeal. Successive visitations of famine and plague have in many places so crippled the finances of these boards that they have had the greatest difficulty in averting a complete breakdown, and it was a serious reproach to existing arrangements that, while there was such a plethora of money in the Government of India's Treasury, and even Provincial Governments were not able to exhaust all the grants made to them, these Local Bodies, whose work concerns the health and comfort of the public far more intimately than that of either the Supreme or the Provincial Governments, should continue year after year in a state almost verging on bankruptcy, and should be unable to discharge satisfactorily even their most elementary duties! Government have now come forward to assist in a liberal spirit the District and Local Boards, and the assistance will evoke the sincere gratitude of these boards. Municipal Bodies have for the present been left out in the cold, but the principle of admitting Local Bodies to a share in the financial prosperity of Government having once been accepted, I venture to think that assistance, similar to what has now been offered to District and Local Boards, cannot reasonably be withheld from municipalities, whose difficulties are not less serious, and whose duties are even more onerous than those of the boards. . . .

The Need for Agricultural Relief

'The Indian agricultural producer is terribly handicapped, and his position is getting harder every day. In the first place, nowhere is the burden of taxes on the land in relation to produce so heavy as in this country. . . . While elsewhere the total burden on land is well below 10 per cent. of the gross produce, with us, taking the land-revenue alone, we see that the assessment over most areas is about 15 per cent and in some portions as high as 20 per cent of the gross produce; —and this according to official estimates.

'Secondly, everywhere in India, and particularly in the temporarily-settled districts, the utter resourcelessness of the agricultural classes is the most distressing fact of the situation. The cultivator has no capital and has but little credit, and is simply unable to make proper use of Nature's wealth that lies at his door, with the result that his cultivation is of the rudest and most exhausting type. The yield of the soil has been steadily diminishing, except in irrigated tracts, being simply eight to nine bushels an acre, about the lowest yield in the world.

'Thirdly, the currency legislation of Government has hit the rayat very hard, depreciating at once the value of his small savings in silver, and increasing steadily, as prices are adjusting themselves to the new rupee, the burden of his assessment and his debts.

'Fourthly, a succession of bad seasons during the last fifteen years has borne him down with crushing pressure, the MacDonnell Commission observing that the past decade in most parts of India has been "a decade of misfortune and distress."

'Lastly there is his terrible indebtedness, which is admitted by everybody, and which, there is reason to fear, is steadily on the increase.

'In such a situation the struggling rayat, toiling ceaselessly without heart and without hope, needs every assistance and relief that can possibly be brought to him. But the operations of the Settlement Department are going on apace; and everywhere a fresh revision means a fresh enhancement of the Government demand. Taking Madras, Bombay, the Central Provinces, and the United Provinces of Agra and Oudh together we find that during the last ten years the land-revenue collections have risen from 14·4 crores in 1893–4 to 15·4 crores in 1903–4, an increase of fully one crore in ten years. And yet all these provinces have suffered during the period from a succession of calamitous seasons.

'The fearful poverty and indebtedness of the agriculturalist calls for a great and comprehensive scheme of ameliorative action, and no mere palliatives will be of much avail. A general reduction of the State demand in the temporarily-settled provinces, as suggested by Mr. O'Connor, the grant of Permanent Settlement to those provinces, together with a bold scheme for the composition of the rayat's liabilities—nothing less than these measures will really save him from utter and hopeless ruin. The present financial position, with an assured excess of at least 7½ crores of revenue over expenditure, gives Government a great opportunity, which, if allowed to slip now, may never present itself again. A reduction of 20 per cent in the State demand in the Provinces of Madras, Bombay, the Central Provinces, and the United Provinces, will not cost more than 3 crores a year, and the amount sacrificed will return to the State tenfold in the increased prosperity and contentment of the people. And a great scheme for the composition of debts, similar to the one for buying out the landlords in the Irish Land Purchase Act of last year—when the Imperial Treasury undertook to advance a hundred millions sterling for the purpose—will mean the making of the rayat again, and is the only way in which the problem of agricultural indebtedness can be successfully grappled with. . . .

Need for the Associating of Indians in the Work of Government

'A succession of great statesmen, who in their day represented the highest thought and feeling of England, have declared that, in their opinion, England's greatest work in India is to associate the people of this country, slowly it may be, but steadily, with the work of their own Government. To the extent to which this work is accomplished, will England's claim to our gratitude and attachment be real. If, on the other hand, this purpose is ever lost sight of or repudiated, much good work which has already been done will be destroyed, and a position created which must fill all true well-wishers of both England and India with a feeling of deep anxiety.'

This speech (the Budget speech of 1905) will be seen upon detailed examination to have laid down principles and indicated lines of policy, many of which have been followed with remarkable exactness in the subsequent evolution of India towards self-government. That this is so, is a tribute not merely to Gokhale's political sagacity and to his grasp of the realities of the situation in regard to his country's future, but to his own force and effectiveness in advocating the right lines of advance. He not only showed how progress was to be attained, he ensured by his constant wise pressure that progress along those lines became an actual fact; and his influence in this respect lasted far beyond the short limits of his own lifetime.

President of the Poona Municipality

His reference to the difficulties of Indian municipalities is especially worthy of note. He himself was President of the Poona Municipality for several years, and knew well the disadvantages and handicaps which hinder the progress of Indian municipal life. In that capacity he showed a power of vigorous administration, which made his tenure of office memorable. The work of the municipal meetings over which he presided was done with thoroughness and despatch. He introduced a system by which the members of the municipality were permitted to interrogate the executive officers at the meetings on points of administration—the same system, in other words, of which he himself was to make such effective use in the Imperial Council after the introduction of the Minto-Morley reforms. He also introduced a rule that the minutes of the municipal meetings should be printed and circulated to the members. His services to Poona as president of the municipality made it plain that Gokhale was no mere academic critic of other people's methods of administration, who would himself be helpless in a position of responsibility; but that he was a vigorous and practical administrator, able to translate his ideals into effective action.

VIII

1905 (*Contd.*)

The Servants of India Society

THE year 1905 was an important one in Gokhale's career, not merely because in that year he made the greatest of all his Budget speeches—the great utterance from which quotation has just been taken—but also because in that year he became President of the Indian National Congress, the highest honour to which a patriotic Indian aspires, whilst in 1905 also he founded the Servants of India Society.

This organisation, which was, and in large measure still is, a practical embodiment of Gokhale's spirit, and a means for the permanent expression of his beliefs and ideals, was originally founded in imitation of the organisation of the Jesuits.[1] At first it was a complete autocracy, under the control of Gokhale himself, but later its constitution was changed in order to provide for its control by a body of three, with a president and a secretary. This body is responsible for the admission of new members. Candidates for admission must be well educated, and men of character and enthusiasm. They undergo a course of training extending over five years, the first two or three of which are spent in economic and social studies, and the rest in practical work, for example

[1] See Paranjpye, *op. cit.*, p. 65.

in famine relief or in the founding and assisting of co-operative credit societies. Members receive an allowance beginning at Rs. 50 (about £3 10*s*.) per mensem, rising eventually to Rs. 125, and are not allowed to augment this pittance by earning money privately. Any income which their activities bring in goes into the general funds of the society. The central headquarters of the society is at Poona, where there is a fine building with an excellent library.

During the eventful years which have passed since its foundation the society has done yeoman service for India in a large variety of spheres, and its leaders have been leaders also in the national life—men who have shared to a remarkable degree in their founder's gift of wise, broad-spirited and constructive statesmanship.

Gokhale wrote the following preamble to the rules of the Society:

'For some time past, the conviction has been forcing itself on many earnest and thoughtful minds that a stage has been reached in the work of nation-building in India, when for further progress the devoted labours of a specially trained agency, applying itself to its task in true missionary spirit, are required. The work that has been accomplished so far has indeed been of the highest value. The growth during the last fifty years of a feeling of common nationality, based upon common traditions and ties, common hopes and aspirations, and even common disabilities, has been most striking. The fact that we are Indians first and Hindus, Muhammadans, and Parsees or Christians afterwards, is being realised in a steadily increasing measure, and the idea of a united and renovated India, marching onwards to a place among the nations of the world, worthy of her great past, is no longer a mere idle dream in a few imaginative minds, but is the definitely accepted creed of those who form the brain of the community—the educated classes of the country. A creditable beginning has already been made in matters of education and of local self-government; and all classes of the people are slowly but steadily coming under the influence of liberal ideas. The claims of public life are every day receiving wider recognition, and attachment to the land of our birth is growing into a strong and deeply cherished passion of the heart. The annual meetings of congresses and conferences, the work of public bodies and associations, the writings in the columns of the Indian press—all bear witness to the new life that is coursing in the veins of the people. The results achieved so far are undoubtedly most gratifying, but they only mean that the jungle has been cleared and the foundations laid. The great work of rearing the superstructure has yet to be taken in hand, and the situation demands on the part of workers devotion and sacrifices proportionate to the magnitude of the task.

'The Servants of India Society has been established to meet, in some measure, these requirements of the situation. Its members frankly accept the British connection as ordained, in the inscrutable dispensation of Providence, for India's good. Self-government within the Empire for their country, and a higher life generally for their countrymen is their goal. This goal, they recognize, cannot be attained without years of earnest and patient effort and sacrifice worthy of the cause. Much of the work must be directed towards building up in the country a higher type of character and capacity than is generally available at present, and advance can only be slow. Moreover, the path is beset with great difficulties; there will be constant temptations to turn back; bitter disappointments will repeatedly try the faith of those who have put their hand to the work. But the weary toil can have but one end, if only the workers grow not faint-hearted on the way.

'One essential condition of success in this work is that a sufficient number of our countrymen must now come forward to devote themselves to the cause in the spirit in which religious work is undertaken. Public life must be spiritualized. Love of country must so fill the heart that all else shall appear as of little moment at its side. A fervent patriotism which rejoices at every opportunity of sacrifice for the Motherland, a dauntless heart which refuses to be turned back from its object by difficulty or danger, a deep faith in the purpose of Providence which nothing can shake—equipped with these, the worker must start on his mission and reverently seek the joy which comes of spending oneself in the service of one's country.

'The Servants of India Society will train men prepared to devote their lives to the cause of the country in a religious spirit, and will seek to promote, by all constitutional means, the national interests of the Indian people. Its members will direct their efforts principally towards (1) creating among the people, by example and by precept, a deep and passionate love of the Motherland, seeking its highest fulfilment in service and sacrifice; (2) organizing the work of political education and agitation, basing it on a careful study of public questions, and strengthening generally the public life of the country; (3) promoting relations of cordial goodwill and co-operation among the different communities; (4) assisting educational movements, especially those for the education of women, the education of backward classes, and industrial and scientific education; (5) helping forward the industrial development of the country; (6) the elevation of the depressed classes.

'The headquarters of the society will be at Poona, where it will maintain a home for its members, and, attached to it a library for the study of subjects bearing on its work.'

The pledges taken by a new member joining the society are as follows:

1. That the country will always be first in his thoughts, and that he will give to her service the best that is in him.
2. That in serving the country he will seek no personal advantage for himself.
3. That he will regard all Indians as brothers, and will work for the advancement of all, without distinction of caste and creed.
4. That he will be content with such provision for himself and his family as the society may be able to make, and that he will devote no part of his energies to earning money for himself.
5. That he will lead a pure personal life.

6. That he will engage in no personal quarrel with anyone.

7. That he will always keep in view the aims of the society, and watch over its interests with the utmost zeal, doing all he can to advance its work; and that he will never do anything which is inconsistent with the objects of the society.

It is obvious that in regard to the creation of the Servants of India Society we see an entirely different side to Gokhale's personality from any that we have so far studied. It is a side to his personality, moreover, which strongly differentiates him from any of those European statesmen, and especially from Cavour, with whom one is inclined for this reason and that to compare him.

Here is a man at the height of his powers as a statesman, a man who has shown an entirely exceptional power of practical political skill, a man whose chief subject of study is the dry field of Economics, a man who has for twenty years spent laborious hours daily delving in the midst of Blue Books, and whose activities have earned him the reputation of being a past-master of statistics. Suddenly he reveals in himself a strain of other-worldly idealism. He calls for a body of disciples who will voluntarily abandon all ambition in the ordinary sense, and pledge themselves *in a religious spirit* to a life of toil and sacrifice in the cause of their country.

His Religion

In this account of Gokhale little has been said of his religious beliefs; for he seldom in his public utterances gave expression to them. We know that, while political problems engrossed him, there was never any doubt as to his relation to the movements of his time for the reform of Hinduism and of the Hindu social system. One who reverenced M. G. Ranade as Gokhale reverenced him and for whom, as Mr. Gandhi tells us of him, 'Ranade's authority was final in every matter,'[1] was bound to give its due place to a spirit of sincere religious devotion.

The spirit that inspired much of his political activity is plainly revealed in his plans for this society. He resented strongly in conversation the suggestion that it was a purely secular body, and loved to show its affinity to the religious orders of mediæval Christianity. It is clear that behind Gokhale the mathematician, the professor, the economist, the administrator, the statesman, there lay another Gokhale, Gokhale the idealist, the man of faith and aspiration, scorning all so-called 'practical' limitations of the possible.

His friend, Mr. K. Natarajan, refuses to be satisfied with the designation of 'agnostic' as representing his religious attitude. He quotes a letter written in 1902 which indicates that he was attracted at that time by the 'aims and aspirations' of Swami Vivekananda, and tells how, some years later, Gokhale 'quietly said to him' that he had reached a faith in God as love. His friends, such as the devout theist Sir Ramakrishna Bhandarkar, expected him to make a public declaration of the change in his religious beliefs that had come about; but to their regret, 'that declaration never came.'[2]

[1] Gandhi, *The Story of My Experiments with Truth*, vol. I, p. 539.
[2] Natarajan, *Gopal Krishna Gokhale*, p. 4.

1905 (*Contd.*)

His Work in England

The session of the Indian National Congress held at Benares at the end of the year 1905 was to some extent marred by the divisions which two years later were to come to a head at Surat. Gokhale had to hurry back from England to be its president. He had gone on this, his second visit to England, as a representative of the Congress, deputed to place the grievances of India before the English people, especially with regard to the rule of Lord Curzon. He had remained only fifty days in the country, during which he delivered forty-five public speeches. These speeches were marked by moderation and good sense, although they plainly expressed the resentment which was felt in India at many of Lord Curzon's later measures.

That resentment had centred during recent months in a violent agitation against the partition of the province of Bengal. To this tumult and the deep-seated discontent of which it was a symptom Lord Curzon—as his biographer, Lord Ronaldshay, remarks—'appeared strangely insensible.' He seemed, in thus ignoring a movement of protest so powerful and so widespread, to be governed by a contempt for the educated opinion of India, and to ignore it by a deliberate purpose, such as was believed to lie behind the Universities Act. In these circumstances it seemed necessary that the facts, as they appeared in India, should be brought to the attention of the public in Great Britain; and how unsparing of himself in the discharge of this duty to his country Gokhale was, may be gathered from what he says in a letter written from Manchester in November, 1905. By that time Lord Curzon had felt compelled, because of the dispute over military policy which had arisen between him and Lord Kitchener, to resign the Viceroyalty, and Lord Minto had been appointed as his successor. When Gokhale wrote, his visit to England was nearing its close.

'This is my last letter to you from England; and in five days more I shall leave for Marseilles. As the time of my departure approaches, the pressure of work here is growing so terrible as to drive me almost mad. During the last five days, would you believe it, I have been working seventeen and eighteen hours a day. I should have thought such a thing incredible, had I not myself been going through it. Every evening I have to address a meeting, and sometimes two meetings. And to-day I have to address three meetings here. Then interviews have been arranged with a number of prominent men of both sides, and the whole day long I have to be rushing about from one place to another, sometimes without breakfast or lunch or both; and the anxiety of keeping an appointment punctually causes a great worry, owing to long and unfamiliar distances. Then there is heavy, urgent correspondence; and finally there are visits from Anglo-Indians and others to me, all which takes time. Oh, it is terrible—this strain—and it has already told, I am sorry to tell you, on my poor health. However, thank God, it will be over in five days more.'

President of the Indian National Congress

So seriously had his hard work in England affected Gokhale's health, that he had to undergo an operation on board the steamer which brought him back to India. In spite of this, he hurried off to Benares in order to preside at the Congress. His Presidential Address contained the following passages:

Lord Curzon

'How true it is that to everything there is an end! Thus even the Viceroyalty of Lord Curzon has come to a close! For seven long years all eyes had constantly to turn to one masterful figure in the land—now in admiration, now in astonishment, more often in anger and in pain, till at last it has become difficult to realize that a change has really come. For a parallel to such an administration we must, I think, go back to the times of Aurangzeb in the history of our own country. There we find the same attempt at a rule excessively centralized and intensely personal, the same strenuous purpose, the same overpowering consciousness of duty, the same marvellous capacity for work, the same sense of loneliness, the same persistence in a policy of distrust and repression, resulting in bitter exasperation all round.

'I think even the most devoted admirers of Lord Curzon cannot claim that he has strengthened the foundations of British rule in India. . . . It is a sad truth that to the end of his administration he did not really understand the people of India. This was at the root of his many inconsistencies, and made him a perpetual puzzle to most men. And thus the man who professed in all sincerity, before he assumed the reins of office, his great anxiety to show the utmost deference to the feelings, and even the prejudices of those over whom he was set to rule, ended by denouncing in unmeasured terms not only the present generation of Indians, but also their remote ancestors and even the ideals of their race, which they cherish above everything else. He who, in the early part of his administration, publicly warned the official classes that "official wisdom is not so transcendent as to be superior to the stimulus and guidance of public opinion," and who declared that in the present state of India "the opinion of the educated classes is one which it is not statesmanlike to ignore or to despise," ended by trampling more systematically upon that opinion than any of his predecessors, and claiming for his own judgment and that of his official colleagues a virtual character of infallibility.

The Partition of Bengal

'The question that is uppermost in the minds of us all at this moment is the Partition of Bengal. A cruel wrong has been inflicted on our Bengalee brethren, and the whole country has been stirred to its deepest depths with sorrow and resentment, as has never been the case before. The scheme of partition, concocted in the dark and carried out in the face of the fiercest opposition that any Government measure has encountered during the last half-a-century, will always stand as a complete illustration of the worst features of the present system of bureaucratic rule—its utter contempt for public opinion, its arrogant pretensions to superior wisdom, its reckless disregard of the most cherished feelings of the people, the mockery an appeal to its sense of justice becomes, its cool preference of Service interests to those of the governed.

The Goal of the Congress

'The goal of the Congress is that India should be governed in the interests of the Indians themselves, and that, in course of time, a form of Government should be attained in this country similar to what exists in the Self-Governing Colonies of the British Empire. For better, for worse, our destinies are now linked with those of England; and the Congress freely recognizes that whatever advance we seek must be within the Empire itself. That advance, moreover, can only be gradual, as at each stage of the progress it may be necessary for us to pass through a brief course of apprenticeship before we are enabled to go on to the next one; for it is a reasonable proposition that the sense of responsibility required for the proper exercise of the political institutions of the West, can be acquired by an Eastern people through practical training and experiment only. To admit this is not to express any agreement with those who usually oppose all attempts at reform on the plea that the people are not ready for it. "It is liberty alone," says Mr. Gladstone with profound wisdom, "which fits men for liberty. This proposition, like every other in politics, has its bounds; but it is far safer than the counter doctrine, Wait till they are fit." While, therefore, we are prepared to allow that an advance towards our goal may be only by reasonably cautious steps, what we emphatically insist on is that the resources of the country should be primarily devoted to the work of qualifying the people by means of education and in other ways for such an advance. Even the most bigoted champion of the existing system of administration will not pretend that this is in any degree the case at present. Our net revenue is about 44 millions sterling. Of this very nearly one-half is now eaten up by the Army. The Home Charges, exclusive of their military portion, absorb nearly one-third. The two, between them, account for about 34 millions out of 44. Then over three millions are paid to European officials in civil employ. This leaves only about seven millions at the disposal of the Government to be applied to other purposes.

'Can anyone who realises what this means wonder that the Government spends only a miserable three-quarters of a million out of State funds on the education of the people—primary, secondary and higher, all put together! . . . We have now been a hundred years under England's rule, and yet to-day four villages out of every five are without a school-house, and seven children out of eight are allowed to grow up in ignorance and in darkness? Militarism, Service interests, and the interests of English capitalists, all take precedence to-day of the true interests of the Indian people in the administration of the country. Things cannot be otherwise; for it is the government of the people of one country by the people of another, and this, as Mill points out, is bound to produce great evils.

'Now the Congress wants that all this should be governed, first and foremost, in the interests of the Indians themselves. This result will be achieved only in proportion as we obtain more and more voice in the Government of our country. We are prepared to bear—and bear cheerfully—our fair share of the burdens of the Empire, of which we are now a part, but we want to participate in the privileges also, and we object most strongly to being sacrificed, as at present, in order that others may prosper.

'Then the Congress asks for a redemption of those promises for the equal treatment of Indians and Englishmen in the government of this country, which have been so solemnly given us by the Sovereign and the Parliament of England. It is now three-quarters of a century since the Parliament passed an Act, which, the Court of Directors pointed out, meant that there was to be no governing caste in India. The governing caste, however, is still as vigorous, as exclusive as ever.

'No one denies that a large proportion of the members of the bureaucracy bring to their work a high level of ability, a keen sense of duty, and a conscientious desire, within the limits of the restricted opportunities permitted by the predominance of other interests, to do what good they can for the people. It is the system which is really at fault—a system which relegates the interest of the people to a very subordinate place, and which, by putting too much power into the hands of these men, impairs their sense of responsibility and develops in them a spirit of intolerance of criticism.

THE PROGRAMME FOR THE IMMEDIATE FUTURE

'I would most earnestly and respectfully suggest that we should select such reforms as may be immediately urged with the greatest effect, and press them forward in this country and in England with all the energy we can command. In my humble opinion, our immediate demands should be: (1) A reform of our Legislative Councils, i.e., raising the proportion of elected members to one-half, requiring the budgets to be formally passed by the Councils, and empowering the members to bring forward amendments, with safeguards for bringing the debates to a close in a reasonable time. The Presidents of the Councils should have the power of Veto. . . . (2) The appointment of at least three Indians to the Secretary of State's Council, to be returned, one each by the three older provinces. (3) The creation of Advisory Boards in all Districts throughout India, whom the heads of Districts should be bound to consult in important matters of administration concerning the public, before taking action. For the present, their function should be only advisory, the Collectors or District Magistrates being at liberty to set aside their advice at their discretion. (4) The recruitment of the judicial branch of the Indian Civil Service from the legal profession in India. (5) The separation of Judicial and Executive functions. (6) A reduction of military expenditure. (7) A large extension of primary education. (8) Facilities for industrial and technical education. (9) An experimental measure to deal with the indebtedness of the peasantry over a selected area. . . .

'The real moral interest of a struggle such as we are engaged in lies not so much in the particular readjustment of present institutions which we may succeed in securing, as in the strength that the conflict brings us to be a permanent part of ourselves. The whole life of a people, which is broader and deeper than what is touched by purely political institutions, is enriched even by failures, provided the effort has been all that it should be. For such enrichment the present struggle is invaluable. "The true end of our work," Mr. Ranade said nine years ago, "is to renovate, to purify, and also to perfect the whole man by liberating his intellect, elevating his standard of duty, and developing to the full all his powers. Till so renovated, purified, and perfected, we can never hope to be what our ancestors once were—a chosen people, to whom great tasks were allotted, and by whom great deeds were performed. Where this feeling animates the worker, it is a matter of comparative indifference in what particular direction it asserts itself, and in what particular method it proceeds to work. With a liberated manhood, with buoyant hope, with a faith that never shirks duty, with a sense of justice that deals fairly by all, with unclouded intellect and powers fully cultivated, and lastly, with a love that overleaps all bounds, renovated India will take her proper rank among the nations of the world, and be the master of the situation and of her own destiny. This is the end to be reached—this is the promised land. Happy are they who see it in distant vision; happier those who are permitted to work and clear the way on to it; happiest they who live to see it with their eyes and tread upon the holy soil once more. Famine and pestilence, oppression and sorrow, will then be myths of the past, and the gods will once more again descend to the earth and associate with men, as they did in times which we now call mythical."

'I can add nothing that may be worthy of being placed by the side of these beautiful words. I will only call to your minds the words of another great teacher of humanity, who asks us to keep our faith in spite of trying circumstances, and warns us against the presumption of despairing because we do not see the whole future clearly before our eyes:

Our times are in His hand
Who saith "A whole I planned,
Youth shows but half; trust God: see all, nor be afraid."'

Gokhale's judgment on Lord Curzon's viceroyalty was inevitably severe, for the policy that he pursued with a resolution not less stubborn than Lord Curzon's own brought them into sharp conflict with each other. But Gokhale was far too generous a man to fail to do justice to the high qualities of his opponent.

In his *Life of Lord Curzon*, Lord Ronaldshay tells us that six months after his Congress speech, 'when Lord Curzon himself lay stricken with the pain of a great affliction,' Mr. Gokhale wrote to him that the heart of all India would go out to him in profound and reverent sorrow. And he spoke in touching terms of the inevitable loneliness of 'such rare spirits as your Lordship who live for lofty ends and make a religion of all their work.'[1]

Soon Gokhale found it necessary to visit Great Britain once more and resume his efforts there to explain the causes that lay behind the agitation that continued to distract India. He had declared in his address to Congress that 'the tremendous upheaval of popular feeling that had taken place in Bengal . . . would constitute a landmark in the history of national progress.' This upheaval had not in any respect subsided in spite of the repressive measures of the head of the new province that had been formed, Sir Bamfylde Fuller. The situation eventually resulted in the resignation of the Lieutenant-Governor, in regard to whom Lord Morley in his *Reminiscences* makes the comment, 'He is . . . I fear, no more

[1] Ronaldshay, *Life of Curzon*, vol. II, p. 390.

fitted to manage the state of things in East Bengal than I am to drive an engine.'

The importance of the work that Gokhale was able to do for his country may be judged from the following letters written from England during his stay there. The first was written in May, 1906:

'This Bengal business has kept me busy the whole of this week, and I am glad to tell you that I have been able to do some useful work. On Monday last I had a long and most cordial interview with Mr. Ellis, the Under-Secretary of State for India, in regard to the matter, and yesterday I had an equally cordial and equally satisfactory interview with Mr. Morley.[1] I am leaving to-morrow morning for Gloucester—Sir W. Wedderburn's place— and from there I go to Liverpool to address public meetings, returning to London on the 16th instant. And Mr. Morley has asked me to see him again on my return from Liverpool.

'I may tell you for your information only that I made a passionate appeal to Mr. Morley yesterday to realize the great responsibility of his teachings in his present office. And he was much moved, and he spoke very freely of his difficulties and his intentions. You will be able to judge how cordial and satisfactory the interview was from the fact that when I expressed the hope before parting that if Bengal affairs took up most of our time at the next interview, and I was not able to lay before Mr. Morley the proposals of reform that I have come here to press on his attention, he would give me a third chance of seeing him, he said: "It is not a question, Mr. Gokhale, of how many interviews I would grant you, but of how many *you* would give me. And if you are equal to ten interviews, I would like to have all ten of them."'

Writing two months later, on the 6th of July, he continues his account of his 'day to day struggle':

[1] Mr. (afterwards Lord) Morley was now Secretary of State for India.

'I am sorry to tell you that the strain of this work, and more especially the worry involved in it, has begun to tell on my health; and I am again not so well as I was for some time on coming to this country. My principal work here now has practically resolved itself into a tug-of-war with the officials of the India Council as to who should capture Mr. Morley's mind. I am only one; and they are so many; and my opportunities of access to Mr. Morley are far more restricted than theirs; but I am doing all that one man can do, and I really believe that more than what I am doing is not humanly possible in our present circumstances. Next Monday—three days only from now—we shall in all probability have the first result of this tug-of-war. I expect Mr. Morley to make a statement on that day about East Bengal affairs, and I shall be greatly disappointed if Fuller's transfer from that Province is not announced on that day. Such an announcement has been virtually promised to me, and was to have been made on Tuesday last; but the India Office people seem to have again prevailed so far as to secure a postponement of the announcement.

'The worry of this day to day struggle is not dissimilar to that with which we tend a sick person who is hovering between life and death. I have had so far five interviews with Mr. Morley, and three with his Under-Secretary, Mr. Ellis. And two weeks ago, finding the strength of adverse influences at work to be extremely great, I made up my mind to substitute a flank movement for the frontal attack which I was till then making. I told Mr. Morley freely that as his position was most difficult between two sets of conflicting representations, the best way out of the difficulty was to appoint a Royal Commission, consisting, say, of seven men, to go out to India and enquire whether the present association of the people with the administration of their own affairs was adequate, considering the spread of education in the country, and if not what measures might be adopted to make it adequate. There should be two Anglo-Indian officials on this Commission, two men from our side (one of them should be Sir W. Wedderburn and the other an Indian) and three independent English politicians (one being Unionist and the other two good Liberals, to give the Commission a slightly predominant Liberal character, as it was a Liberal Government that would be appointing it).

'The proposal has been very favourably received by Mr. Morley, and he is considering it at present. I want him to make an announcement on this subject on 20th July. If he does that, and if he removes Fuller and Emerson from their present positions before that, and if he appoints Mr. Dutt to his Council at an early date, public feeling in India will, I think, be conciliated to some extent; and while the Commission is holding its enquiry, Mr. Morley will have time to study the different questions for himself. The Commission will give him the two things that he wants at the present moment—time, and a definite lead.

'I have kept this proposal, as far as possible, confidential, because, if a Commission is to be appointed, it should appear as coming from Mr. Morley himself rather than that he has yielded to a demand. And I have mentioned it in this letter because it won't reach you before the 20th and the fate of the proposal will have been decided by then.

'All my time is taken up now in coaching different Members of Parliament in connection with the forthcoming Budget debate. We have drafted ten notices of motions covering all our principal grievances, and I think we shall have for the first time our case properly and fully presented before Parliament.'

IX

1907–1909

THE SALT TAX

THE Budget speech of 1906, which was a very fine one, covered much the same ground as previous utterances, though in a fresh manner. In the course of his Budget speech of 1907 Gokhale dealt, as he had frequently done before, with the question whether the salt tax really imposed a heavy burden on the poor. He welcomed a reduction in the tax, which the Finance Minister had foreshadowed, but argued convincingly against his claim that the tax did not 'press with undue severity upon the poor' and that it was the only contribution towards the public expenditure made by a large number of people. His claim was that the poorer classes contributed, 'relatively to their resources, much more than their fair share to the revenues of the State.' He was the more urgent in pressing his point of view in this matter, as Mr. Morley had hinted that they might look forward to a time when this tax might be done away with altogether.

FREE PRIMARY EDUCATION

In regard to another policy which he was unwearied in urging upon the attention of Government, that of Free Primary Education, he spoke as follows:

'I now come to what is in some respects the most gratifying feature of the present Budget—I mean the statement which the Hon. Member makes on the subject of Free Primary Education. The statement is brief, but it says enough to indicate clearly the resolute purpose that lies behind it. The whole country has reason to feel grateful to Your Lordship's Government for taking up this question in this earnest spirit. The circular letter of November last and this paragraph in the financial statement, taken together, leave no doubt in my mind that before the Budget for next year is presented, primary education will have been made free throughout India; for I cannot imagine any Local Government standing in the way of the adoption of this measure, since the Government of India is going to find all the money required for it . . .'

THE BUREAUCRACY

He then proceeded:

'The question, however, that in my humble opinion transcends all others in importance at this moment is how to associate the people of this country with the administration of their own affairs, so that their growing estrangement may be prevented, and, while their self-respect is satisfied on one side, the bond between them and the Empire may be strengthened on the other. The Englishman who imagines that India can be governed much longer on the same lines as in the past, and the Indian who thinks that he must seek a destiny for his country outside this Empire, of which now, for better or worse, we are a part—both alike show an inadequate appreciation of the realities of the present situation. The main difficulty in regard to this association arises from the fact that the Government of this country is really in the hands of the Civil Service, which is practically a caste, with all the exclusiveness and love of monopoly which characterise castes. I am speaking in the presence of so many distinguished members of that Service, and I respectfully trust that I shall not be considered guilty of rudeness in making these observations.

'These men, who give on the whole a high average of

work, and who moreover feel conscious that they are doing their best, are naturally satisfied with their positions, and they expect us to be satisfied with ours. And as they happen to be practically the sole advisers of both the Viceroy and the Secretary of State, no reform which they do not approve has, as a rule, any chance of being adopted. Of course there are exceptions, but I am speaking now of the Service as a class. . . .

The Urgent Need of Reform

'This kind of thing has now gone on for many years, with the result that the attitude of the public mind towards the Government—and "opinion," as Burke calls it, is of greater importance than laws or executive power in maintaining order—has undergone a steady and, of late years, even a rapid change. Since last year the impression has prevailed that the Government has at last decided to move forward, and that important concessions are contemplated. I earnestly trust that this impression is well-founded. I trust also that the proposed reforms, when announced, will be found to be substantial, and conceived in a generous spirit.

'It is of importance that there should be no unnecessary delay in this matter. The public mind is in a state of great tension, and unless the concessions are promptly announced, and steps taken to give immediate effect to them, they will I fear, lose half their efficacy and all their grace. The situation is an anxious—almost a critical one; and unless the highest statesmanship inspires the counsels of the Government, difficulties threaten to arise of which no man can foresee the end.'[1]

[1] The attitude of Gokhale towards the members of the Government whose measures he had so consistently to criticise and oppose is indicated in the following passage from the *Letters to Nobody* of Sir Guy Fleetwood Wilson who was Finance Member from 1908 to 1913.

'The one man I frankly feared was Gokhale, the Gladstone of India. Accordingly I endeavoured to find out what Gokhale's line of attack would be. All and everyone told me that the attempt would be futile, and that any apparent frankness on Gokhale's part would only be a cloak to his real intentions. So I left him severely alone.

'Imagine my surprise at receiving on the eve of the debate a letter from Gokhale, whom I did not even know, to the effect that as he

1907–1909

The Bengal Disturbances

The grave necessities of the public situation demanded that Gokhale should almost immediately return once more to Great Britain. Crimes of violence went on increasing both in Bengal and in other parts of India during 1907 and 1908. At the same time the policy to which both the Viceroy, Lord Minto, and the Secretary of State, Mr. Morley, were committed was one of political progress and reform. There was always the danger lest a policy of reaction should be resorted to in order to counter the forces of violence. The activities of Mr. B. G. Tilak, too, in Western India were scarcely less disturbing to the authorities than the anarchist movement in Bengal; and in June, 1908, he was arrested and found guilty of sedition. In these circumstances there was plenty for Gokhale to do in England, and how he laboured in the cause of his country we can learn from letters written to his friends in India during the six months, from May till October, spent by him in England.

He reached London early in May and almost immediately thereafter he wrote as follows:

'On landing at Marseilles, we saw in the papers the news of the latest developments in Bengal, and of course since then we have been feeling most anxious about the situation.[1] . . . (I fear there will now be a fierce outburst of repression, and for the next two or three years it will be a case of repression

had good reason to believe that I meant to do my utmost for the good of India, he had no desire to embarrass me, and that therefore he sent me the notes of the speech he proposed to make so that I should not be taken unawares.

'I do not believe that such a generous attitude has ever been assumed by the Leader of the Opposition in any other country in the world.'

[1] Two English ladies were killed at Muzafferpur by a bomb intended for the Magistrate.

on one side and crime on the other. Ultimately, I have no doubt, crime will be stamped out, or the violence of the extreme section of the extremists will get exhausted; but meanwhile men like ourselves can do very little useful work, and we shall be compelled merely to helplessly look on.) I expect to see Lord Morley next week, and I mean to tell him freely what I think of the situation.

'I am extremely sorry that I should be out of India at such a grave juncture. There is really some fatality connected with my visits to this country. Every time I come here, something happens in India to throw the country into a state of wild excitement. Just now I am feeling anxious, not merely as to what fresh developments may take place in India, but also as to how the several members of our Society will comprehend the true character of the present crisis, and conduct themselves so as to prevent any harm coming to the Society. You must all realize that whatever the shortcomings of the bureaucracy, and however intolerable at times the insolence of individual Englishmen, they alone stand to-day in the country for order; and without continued order no real progress is possible for our people. It is not difficult at any time to create disorder in our country—it was our portion for centuries—but it is not so easy to substitute another form of order for that which has been evolved by Englishmen in the course of a century. You must all conduct yourselves at this time with the utmost caution and restraint, and let no thoughtless word be uttered publicly or in private which may be misconstrued.'

Lord Morley's Reforms

A fortnight later, he writes:

'Considering the situation I am glad to say that my work is going on very well. My interview with Lord Morley last Friday was an important one, and it was very satisfactory. I was with him for about an hour and fifteen minutes, and we parted with a good understanding. He has promised to consult me freely at every stage of the progress of the Reform proposals, and he has assured me that before the year is over the reforms would be not only formulated, but carried out. Of course this is strictly private, and you must see to it that it does not appear in any of the papers.

'The bomb outrages have no doubt in one sense strengthened the party of repression and reaction among the officials, but for the present at any rate Lord Morley is firm, and he is determined to make the reforms substantial ones. Only, should there unhappily be any further outrages, the Secretary of State will find it impossible to proceed with his reform proposals, and in that event I fear Lord Morley will resign, and another man, whose instinct is not so decisively against coercion, will take his place. An Explosives Act, and a stringent Press Act are of course now inevitable; and I fear they will be added to the Statute Book before this letter reaches you. But Lord Morley is sincerely anxious that repression should not go beyond this, though it is not improbable that he may be rendered powerless to prevent it by the developments in India.

'I would like to know what in your opinion and that of our other members is likely to be the effect of these outrages and the repressive measures which will now be adopted on the fortunes of the two parties in India. Kindly write in detail, and also ask some of the others to write.

'Last Tuesday Mr. Dutt and I had a very useful conference with about forty members of the Indian Parliamentary Committee. I have also seen a considerable number of M.Ps. since coming here, and next week I am to have a conference with five members of the India Council at the India Office. This will be very useful; and I am glad to find the whole atmosphere so friendly to me personally. I have already seen these five members separately, and have discussed the situation freely with them; but the joint conference is Mr. Morison's idea, and I think it will materially help my work.

'One of the most interesting functions at which I have ever been present was a dinner given to me by Mr. Nevinson last week, at which twelve leading Liberal journalists of London and Manchester were present. After I had once responded in the usual way to the toast about my health, I was asked to speak again and explain my programme in detail.

I then spoke for half an hour, and was heard with the greatest kindness. And more than one person has said to me that it was valuable work done. Sir W. Wedderburn, who is delighted with the function, describes it as getting at the brain of the Liberal Party in London. Mr. Massingham and Mr. Gardiner, two of the foremost Liberal editors in London, congratulated me very warmly, and assured me that they had been "profoundly" impressed by what I had said. It is not quite the right thing that I should mention such things myself, but I know they will give you and the other members pleasure, and I lay aside my natural hesitation. All that I remember of the speech is that I spoke with deep feeling, and that I was all the time unconscious of my own existence or of that of the audience.

'I am going to put myself to-morrow into the hands of a specialist. I hope his verdict will not be very depressing. In any case, I mean to do all I can for my poor health while I am here.

'This letter will happily reach you on 12th June—the third anniversary of our beloved Society. I trust you all will be in the home on that day, and I shall be with you in spirit, though physically far away. I trust only one thought will be uppermost in your minds on that day—how you can devote your best energies to building up the strength of the Society, so that the Society may in the fulness of time fulfil its mission of achieving the salvation of our Motherland. May your faith in your work be firm and may the Divine blessing rest on you all, will be my prayer on that day, as in fact it is every day. My vision was never clearer than to-day that we are working on right lines. May you all see with equal clearness, so that all doubts should vanish and no difficulties ever daunt you. Be you to one another as more than brothers, and watch over the interests of the Society, as a mother guards her children, with every throb of your hearts.

'Write and tell me what programme of studies the different members fix upon this session.'

The following letter is dated 19th June:

'This has been a very busy week for me, and I fear the

next week will also be the same. Last Tuesday the expected conference with four members of the India Council and the Under-Secretary for India took place, and I think it was most useful work done. As I believe I have already told you, the four members present were Sir Lawrence Jenkins, Sir Walter Lawrence, Mr. Morison and Mr. Bilgrami. Mr. Gupta was not there. Mr. Buchanan, the Under-Secretary, took a good deal of interest in the proceedings. He is an able man, and is slowly acquiring influence in Indian matters. I had drawn up and circulated beforehand among the members a note of what reforms should be immediately granted, and that note formed the basis of our discussion. It is of course impossible to give you an adequate idea of what took place at the conference in this letter. The proceedings were naturally confidential; but you may take it from me that it has strengthened our position in the India Council in the matter of the forthcoming reforms.'

Tilak's Prosecution

Throughout all his political career Gokhale had found himself in conflict with B. G. Tilak, and had been at pains to dissociate himself from the extreme views which Tilak promulgated. As a consequence he had to endure much misrepresentation by the followers of his more popular rival. The letter which follows shows how great a strain this put upon his patience:

'Your letter of the 4th reached me here last Monday. That letter and two others, which I received by the same mail, left no doubt in my mind that the limits of forbearance had been reached, and that further patience was only another form of cowardice. I felt strongly that I owed it not merely to myself and those who were associated with me, but also to public life in India that the miserable miscreants who made it their business to sit down deliberately and concoct malignant falsehoods against me and others must not be left severely alone any longer; and so I wired to Mr. Dravid to serve lawyers' notices on all such journals as had made or given currency to the dastardly and detestable accusation that I was at the bottom of Mr. Tilak's prosecution.

'I wired to Nateshrao, because from your letter it appeared that you might just now be at Jamkhandi, and I wanted action to be taken at once. I had asked Mr. Dravid to wire back to me what he had done, but unfortunately up to the hour of writing this no wire has been received. I hope this is due not to any feeling of hesitation in the matter but simply because it required time to find out what journals had offended and to serve lawyers' notices on them. As I have said in the wire, I want *complete and immediate* retractation, and by way of showing the sincerity of their regret, they must make substantial contributions (not less than Rs. 500 in any case, and more according to a journal's position and its offence) to charitable institutions. The two institutions for which I would like whatever payments are realized to go are Mr. Shinde's Mission for the Depressed Classes and Mr. Karve's Home.[1] I understand that even the first paragraph in the *Bande Mataram* is a libel, as no one has a right to publish such injurious "suspicions." I am told, though I have not seen it myself, that the *Kesari* had quoted the paragraph from the *Bande Mataram.* If so, you must serve a notice on the *Kesari*, too. I expect most of the journals will come down as soon as they get notices. Such of them as do not do so will have to be proceeded against in December, when I arrive. As I have told you before, the whole accusation in a despicable and malevolent fabrication. I never had any talk whatever with Lord M. about Mr. Tilak before the prosecution. I had a talk with him afterwards, and in that I expressed my deep regret at the prosecution, and pointed out its great unwisdom; and I know as a fact that Lord M. was himself greatly distressed when he heard about Mr. T.'s arrest, though of course this must be kept confidential. He felt, as we all felt, that the chances of his forthcoming reforms conciliating the people in a substantial degree had been largely reduced by this prosecution. Not only this, there is more; but I don't like to write about it. I hear that in Bombay people were saying

[1] A Home for widows.

at the time of the trial (I had this from Mr. Khaparde, who came to see me here the other day) that Sir George Clarke[1] was over-ruled in the matter by his two colleagues, and that Lord M. supported the latter. *Don't believe a word of the story.* It is not true.

'I don't mind confessing that I have been feeling somewhat sad since despatching that telegram on Monday last. During all these years of public life I have often been pursued by similar malevolence, but hitherto I have succeeded in ignoring the attacks. Somehow I feel that I have not been quite loyal to the teachings and principles of my departed master[2] in asking you to proceed against the offending journals as I have done. But though the heart is sad, the brain tells me that the course I have urged is the only course now left open to me. Our public is so gullible that it simply swallows such stories; and the public mind is at present so inflamed that it is positively dangerous, not only for me and mine, but for those who, like the members of our Society, are closely associated with me, and for our work that such odious accusations should be allowed to circulate.'

The Announcement of the Reforms

The fruition of his strenuous toil was now about to be realised and the announcement of the Reforms was imminent. He writes on 30th October:

'In five weeks from to-day I shall sail from Marseilles. Meanwhile, as the day on which the new Reforms will be announced is drawing nearer, the tension on my mind is growing more intolerable. You must have already heard that there is to be a new Royal Proclamation on 2nd November, and according to present intentions Lord Morley's promised statement will be made in the House of Lords on 15th or 20th November, if not earlier. . . .

'I expect the statement will be satisfactory to our side in

[1] The Governor of Bombay. The prosecution of Mr. Tilak was at the instance of the Government of Bombay.

[2] Mr. Ranade is presumably meant.

India. I think we shall in substance get all I have asked for in that confidential note of which I sent N. a copy last month. Here and there there will be alterations, for instance as regards electorates-new Electoral Colleges may be created for each Division, and these colleges may be built up from Taluka boards, so as to secure by a system of proportional representation the adequate representation of minorities. . . .

'The whole scheme will take too long to explain in a letter; but it will be a perfectly fair scheme, similar to those which men like Lord Courtney have been advocating. . . .

'The most important thing is to have an elected majority in Provincial Councils, with the power of passing resolutions on important matters of administration and finance. And this I am now certain we shall get. This means that a machinery will be set up in India which will enable us to advance effectively questions of internal administration, such as free and compulsory primary education, technical education, permanent settlement, agricultural indebtedness and support. The Governor may veto a resolution of the Council once or twice, but he cannot veto it every time; and by building up public opinion behind the Council we shall be able eventually to get our resolutions acted upon. From this to an executive responsible to the Legislative Council is only one step, though a long and difficult step; but in ten years or so that question ought to come within the sphere of practical politics. However, in less than two months I shall be with you, and I can then explain all these things to you. Meanwhile the Reforms, too, will be out before then, and we shall all then know exactly where we stand.

'Parliamentary legislation will be needed to secure a reform of Legislative and Executive Councils; and the Government of India will have to legislate for an extension of local self-government. This latter legislation must be undertaken (at any rate this is what I am insisting on, and trying to secure) during the forthcoming Calcutta Sessions; and if this is secured it will mean that I must be in Calcutta till the end of March. This will necessitate my abandoning my proposed visit to America next March, and my address there to the Civic Forum. But I am not sorry for this, as apart from the opportunity of helping in important legislation, I would like to be in India continuously for some time now in the interests of our Society. It is possible that my presence here may be needed next May for three or four weeks. But about that I shall know definitely by the end of November.'

X

THE MINTO-MORLEY REFORMS

GOKHALE ended the Budget spech of 1908 with memorable words which have already been quoted, but which may be repeated here in the context of the labours and anxieties that called them forth:

> 'Whatever reforms are taken in hand, let them be dealt with frankly and generously. And let not the words, "*too late*," be written on every one of them. For while the Government stands considering—hesitating, receding, debating within itself "to grant or not to grant, that is the question"—opportunities rush past it which can never be recalled. And the moving finger writes, and having writ, moves on.'

The result of such appeals was the granting of the Minto-Morley Reforms, which were announced towards the end of 1908. It cannot be doubted that Gokhale's influence and his explanation of the Indian situation during his stay in England contributed materially to this result. Sir William Wedderburn wrote as follows regarding him in the *Daily News*: 'In no case did he fail to produce a profound and favourable impression by the accuracy of his information and the cogency of his arguments. At personal interviews he was equally successful. To the credit of British statesmen of all parties, it must be recorded that they have all been willing to give a hearing to Mr. Gokhale; and it is no secret that, as Secretary of State for India, Lord Morley accorded to him prolonged interviews, at which he set forth fully the needs and aspirations of the Indian people. The informations thus imparted influenced in no small degree the concessions granted in the Morley-Minto Reforms'.[1]

Probably the most important single provision in the Reforms was the right accorded to members of the Legislative councils of moving resolutions on matters of public importance, and of asking supplementary questions. Gokhale himself, in the few years of life which were left to him was destined to make important use of these newly-acquired rights. It is said that he was offered under the reforms the distinguished honour of being the first Indian member of the Secretary of State's Council. But he believed that he would be able to do better service for his country if he remained at his post as the leader of the Opposition in the Imperial Council; and he regarded as very valuable the independence of speech and outlook which such a position assured to him. In the years which followed he made a more and more effective use of this position, maintaining an implacable hostility to any signs of the spirit of extravagant wastefulness in public expenditure, especially in connection with the Army, tirelessly pressing for a more generous treatment of the 'nation-building departments,' especially sanitation and education, keeping a watchful eye on the status of Indians overseas, and becoming more and more plainly the spokesman of the new India. At the same time he showed all his old spirit of reasonableness and moderation. He never needlessly pressed for a division, and showed a tolerant

[1] Quoted in Shahani, *op. cit.*, p. 180.

willingness to make allowances for his opponents' difficulties. He was even ready to recognise the claims of that mysterious and much-abused entity, 'prestige.'

Gokhale's Speech on the Reforms at the Congress of 1908

At the Indian National Congress, Gokhale spoke as follows in reference to the Reforms:

'Briefly you may say that the Congress has sought three objects during the last twenty-three years. The first may be called a social object—the Congress has sought to promote greater unity among the different elements in this country, and the Congress has sought to promote a greater feeling of nationality throughout the land. . . . To-day the feeling of unity in the country, taking the divergent elements of the country into consideration, is stronger, deeper and more real than it was twenty-three years ago. The same is true of the feeling of nationality. From one end of the country to the other there is a new impulse, a new feeling, a new vibration; and everybody who is interested in the progress of India must rejoice that that feeling of nationality is a true, a deep and a real one in the land to-day. That part however of the work of the Congress we must put aside for the present. But there were two others, and those were objects we had in view with special reference to the influence we sought to exercise on the Government. One was pressing on the attention of the Government specific measures either of improvement or for the redress of grievances, numerous measures to which I am not going to make any reference just now. But the second object underlying all those measures we advocated, and urged by us side by side with them, was to modify as largely as possible the bureaucratic character of the present administration. Now in some respects the most important part of the work of the Congress during these twenty-three years has been the energy expended by it on modifying the bureaucratic administration. And so far as that is concerned, I think we may fairly say that the new measures that have been announced go a long way to effect the modification.

'What are those measures? . . .

Analysis of the Reforms

'At the base we shall have full control over and management of our local affairs. The fabric of local self-government started by Lord Ripon is to be carried to a proper and fitting completion—that itself is a most important thing. Local self-government has been described by many, and very properly described, as a training-ground, a school of political education for our people. We shall have as much scope there for political education as we choose to have. Then as regards the centre, the position will be so largely modified as to amount almost to a revolution. At the present moment in regard to administration it is all confidential reports from subordinate officers to the highest, till at last the top is reached, and we know nothing till the final decision is arrived at and announced; and even if the decision is unfavourable to us or we do not like it, we can only express our regret in our own way and keep still.

'Under the new arrangement all questions affecting everyday administration which involve matters of public importance can be brought in a responsible manner before those in authority in the Legislative councils of the Provinces. In these councils again a non-official majority has been provided for. This non-official majority with the power of raising administrative questions is really an exceedingly important step, and I am quite sure it will very largely modify the bureaucratic character of the existing administration.

'Then in regard to finance our control will be greater.

'Lastly, as regards the seats of the highest power and authority, the Executive Councils, Indians are to be admitted to these councils. They are already on the Secretary of State's Council; and we know what good work is being done by them there. They are to be admitted to the Indian Executive Councils, which means that in formulating policies and determining large questions, racial considerations will recede into the background. The mere presence of Indians will prevent that. Again, the Indian view of questions will be available there; and I expect nothing but good from the appointment of Indians to these councils. Thus we shall have reasonable access to the highest seats of authority; we shall have fair opportunities of exercising influence in matters of Finance and Administration by means of debate; and we shall have got full management of local affairs.

'More than this, a non-official majority in the Provincial councils really means preventive control over Provincial Legislation. We cannot of course pass any law we please, because there is the veto of the Government; but the Government cannot pass any law it pleases without our consent, because we have secured effective control over Provincial legislation.

General Effect of the Reforms

'I have explained in the few observations I have made how things are to-day, and what our position will be when the whole of this scheme is carried into effect. I now come to a few concluding remarks.

'Stated in one sentence, I may describe the change thus. Hitherto we have been engaged in agitation from outside. From now we shall be engaged in what might be called responsible association with the administration, but it *is* association and responsible association in administration. There is plenty of scope for growth here; and as we grow and discharge the responsibilities that devolve on us properly, I am sure there will be progress further and further towards our having what may be called responsible administration. Now these large and generous concessions which have been made by the Government and the Secretary of State must receive at our hands that response which they require. They impose upon us two responsibilities in particular; the first is that a spirit of co-operation with the Government must now be evoked amongst us, instead of mere criticism of Government. The scheme will fail of its purpose, and will prove absolutely useless in practice if our attitude is one of constant antagonism. Therefore the first responsibility that rests upon us is that the scheme should evoke in us a spirit of co-operation with Government. The second is that the new powers should be exercised with moderation and with restraint, and that they should be used solely for the promotion of the interests of the masses of the people. . . .

'Let us therefore not go in pursuit of mere idle dreams and neglect the opportunities which the present offers to us. On the manner in which we, especially the younger section of our countrymen, grow to the height of the new opportunities will depend the future of the country. None of us wants to be satisfied with things as they are. But first we must prove that we can bear these responsibilities before we can ask for any more.

'I have often said, and I repeat it here again, that I do not want any limits, any restrictions, on the growth which should be open to our people. I want the people of our country, men and women, to be able to rise to the full height of their status as men and women of other countries do. But our growth can only be through the discharge of responsibilities; they must first be discharged before we can think of further responsibilities.'

Lord Morley and the Reforms

Gokhale finished his Budget Speech of 1909—the last under the old constitution—with these words:

'That passage in Lord Morley's speech in the House of Lords foreshadowing Mr. Sinha's appointment,[1] with its phrase "one of the King's equal subjects," has touched a chord in Indian hearts which will keep vibrating for some time. It is a passage which will live in the history of this country—in any case it will remain engraved on the hearts of the people. My Lord, I sincerely believe that Your Lordship and Lord Morley have, between you, saved India from drifting towards what cannot be described by any other name than chaos. For, however strong a Government may be, repression never can put down the aspirations of a people and never will.'

[1] Mr. (afterwards Lord) Sinha was appointed a member of the Viceroy's Executive Council.

Gopal Krishna Gokhale

With this year another stage in India's progress was accomplished. Whatever the value of the Morley-Minto Reforms may have been, they gave Gokhale an opportunity of spending himself in his country's cause and of demonstrating his far-seeing wisdom and moderation. His aim was to use the opportunities now gained with a view to further advance. How fully he realised the difficulties that confronted his country, and how he bore himself in face of them, is revealed in a letter written in September of this year from Poona to a correspondent belonging to the Society of Friends in England:

'Our problem,' he writes, 'is indeed an enormously difficult one—I sometimes think that no country in the world was ever called upon to face such a problem as ours. Endless divisions and sub-divisions in the country, the bulk of the population ignorant, and clinging, with a tenacity of which only those who are of them can have an adequate conception, to old modes of thought and sentiment, which are averse to all change and do not understand change, seventy millions of Mohammedans more or less hostile to national aspirations, and all power lodged in the hands of a fleeting body of foreign officials most of whom generally represent your Tory principles at their worst—this is the situation today. Out of this mass an India has to be evolved, strong, free, united, democratic and qualified generally to take her proper place among the nations of the world. It is a task that may well appal and I don't know if it will ever be accomplished. But we can all work towards that end, and after all, there is much in the words of one of your most beautiful hymns—"One step enough for me!"'

XI

1910

The Resolution on Elementary Education

IN 1910, in addition to much other notable work, Mr. Gokhale made an important speech on Elementary Education. He had always given this a primary place in his policy, and he was now able, other immediate objects having been in a measure attained, to press it upon the attention of Government with redoubled energy. He placed before the Imperial Council the following resolution:

'That this Council recommends that a beginning should be made in the direction of making elementary education free and compulsory throughout the country, and that a mixed Commission of officials and non-officials be appointed at an early date to frame definite proposals.

'What is the extent of the problem that we have got to solve in this country? This is the first consideration. Here let me state at the outset that I do not propose compulsion for the present for girls; I propose compulsion only for boys. For girls, for the present and for some years to come, education will have to be on a voluntary basis. In some respects girls' education is even more important than that of boys in the India of to-day, and yet in view of the difficulties that surround that question, that education must be maintained for some years to come only on a voluntary basis. At the same time, far more vigorous efforts are necessary, on that voluntary basis, than have so far been made. But I want the Council clearly to understand that the compulsory principle which I advocate to-day is to be confined only to boys. We must therefore first of all ascertain what would be the number of boys that would be at school if education were compulsory in this country. . . .

'I propose that we should be satisfied with a compulsory period of four years only, as they have in Japan. In Japan the period is from six years to ten years of the child's age. I propose that we should be satisfied with that period.

'If we have this period as the compulsory period, it will be found on a reference to census returns that the proportion of the male population of the country between the years six and ten is less than twelve per cent. of the total male population. Therefore our problem is how to educate, how to have under elementary instruction, twelve per cent. of the male population of the country.

'Now we find that already at the present moment, about three per cent. of the male population is at school—as a reference to the last quinquennial report will show. The number of boys at school, according to that report, is about 36 lakhs; and adding to that number the five or six lakhs that are attending schools not recognised by the State, it will be found that the proportion comes to about three per cent. of the total male population. We, therefore, have one quarter of the male population of school-going age already at school. What we want is to quadruple this attendance and provide for the cost of such quadrupling. Now another reference to the quinquennial report will show that the cost of maintaining all these boys' schools in 1906–7 was about a crore and 36 lakhs, from all sources, provincial, municipal and local, as also fees and other receipts.

'Assuming that all further expansion takes place only out of public funds, that there are no more fees charged, and no more receipts from private sources coming in, we shall need four times this cost in order to have the entire male population of school-going age at school. Four times a crore and 36 lakhs means about 5½ crores; that is, about 4 crores more than what is expended at the present moment will have to be found if the entire male population of school-going age is to be maintained at school.

'Now I do not suggest that the whole of this burden

should fall upon the State. I think it should be divided between the State and local bodies. I would suggest a proportion of two-thirds and one-third, as they have in Scotland, where the Parliamentary grant and the amount spent from local rates stand to each other in the proportion of two to one. If the State will, therefore, undertake to defray two-thirds of this 4 crores, it will mean an additional expenditure of about $2\frac{2}{3}$ crores when every boy is at school, supposing of course that the population remains just what it is now. This, however, it will be seen, will not have to be incurred at once. Two and two-thirds crores will be reached when the entire field has been covered, which will be a slow process, even when the process of compulsion, as I advocate it, has been adopted, because it will have to be applied slowly; I for one shall be satisfied if the whole field is covered in the course of, say, twenty years. If in the course of twenty years we get the entire male population of school-going age at school, I for one shall think that we have done extremely well.

'This means that the whole of this increased cost of $2\frac{2}{3}$ crores which the State will have to incur will be spread over twenty years, and will not be incurred at once.

Actual Proposals

'Having pointed out thus the extent of the problem, I will now come to the actual proposals that I want to make:

'(1) My first proposal is that following the example of the Act of 1870, we should pass an Act conferring powers upon local bodies to make elementary education compulsory in their areas. I recognise, My Lord, that the unpopularity that will be evoked by the principle of compulsion in certain sections will be considerable; and in view of the special circumstances attaching to the position of the British Government in this country, I recognise that this unpopularity should not come to the State on account of any direct compulsion introduced by it. The compulsion introduced therefore should be indirect, through local bodies, and not direct by the State.

'(2) My second proposal is that compulsion should be only for boys, and not for girls.

'(3) My third proposal is that the period of compulsion should be between six years and ten years, as in Japan.

'(4) The fourth proposal is this. In any area where 33 per cent of the male population is already at school, there this principle of compulsion should be applied. I have already pointed out that in England about 43·4 per cent of the children were at school when compulsion was introduced. In Japan about 28 per cent were at school. I should propose 33 per cent as the proportion which should satisfy us that compulsion would not be premature in any particular area. Where 33 per cent of the boys are actually at school, elementary education should be made compulsory for all boys in that area. In other areas the attempt should be to work up to this proportion of 33 per cent. As soon as 33 per cent is reached, compulsion should be introduced.

'(5) My fifth proposal is that wherever compulsory education is introduced it should be gratuitous, because otherwise it would be a great hardship on poor people. At any rate the children of those parents whose income is below a certain limit, say Rs. 25 a month, should receive gratuitous instruction.

'(6) My sixth proposal is that the extra cost should be divided between the Government and the local bodies in the proportion of two to one.

'(7) My seventh proposal is that there should now be a separate Secretary for Education in the Home Department. Instead of having a Director-General I would have a Secretary in the Home Department specially for education, and eventually I look forward to the time when a member in separate charge of education will be included in the Executive Council.

'(8) My eighth proposal is that education should now be a divided head, instead of its being purely a Provincial head. The root of the mischief, as we see it to-day, is there. The resources at the disposal of the Provincial Governments are extremely limited. I know many of the Provincial Governments are anxious to spend more money on primary education; but it is a struggle with them, which they have constantly to carry on, to make the two ends meet; and it is not possible for them to find more money for primary education than they are able to spend at the present moment. The Government of India, on the other hand, has from time to time abundant resources at its disposal, though this year my Hon. Friend has imposed extra taxation. In any case the Government of India has not the same struggle to make its two ends meet that the Local Governments usually have. If it had a direct responsibility for education, instead of the remote responsibility that it has at present, I am quite sure more would be done for education. Education should therefore be a divided charge, and there should be a definite programme before the Government, just as there is a programme for railways, which should be carried out steadily year by year.

'(9) My last proposal in this connection is that a statement describing the progress of education from year to year should be published with the annual Financial Statement, as is done in the case of Army Services and the Railway Board.

'These are the nine definite practical proposals that I would like to submit to the consideration of this Council. I do not claim that these are the details of a complete scheme, they are only general suggestions tentatively thrown out; and if the Council will appoint a Commission such as I suggest, all these suggestions can go to that commission, and the commission would be able to pronounce definitely on their practicability.

Financial Provisions

'I now come to the financial part of the scheme. I have already said that the cost for the State will be about two and two-thirds crores a year, to be worked up to in twenty years. Well, in spite of the financial difficulties of which we have heard a good deal this year, the State is in a position to meet this cost. The resources of the State are ample for this purpose. I will only briefly indicate them. First of all you have the normal growth of revenue, which was once estimated by Sir Edward Baker at about a crore and 20 lakhs a year. Then you must have retrenchment. I trust after what has been said during the course of the recent discussions that a rigorous policy of retrenchment will now be enforced, especially in regard to those departments which show overgrown expenditure, such as the Army and Civil Departments. Thirdly, there is that sum of about a million sterling, which is spent out of revenue, partly for reducing debt under the Famine Insurance Grant, and partly under Railways for redemption of debt. That ought to be made available for expenditure for current purposes. The fourth resource is this. For years in the 'sixties' and 'seventies' our import duties used to be at $7\frac{1}{2}$ per cent instead of 5 per cent. There is no reason why they should not be at $7\frac{1}{2}$ per cent. again. That will bring two and a half crores more for my Hon. Friend there. The fifth source that I would point out is an export duty on jute and on several other commodities. A 5 per cent. duty on jute will mean about a crore of rupees. Lastly I go further and I say this, that if the worst comes to the worst, and every other resource fails, which I do not for a moment think to be possible, I shall be prepared to advocate an extra 8 annas on salt, because I think it is a smaller evil that my countrymen should eat less salt than that their children should continue to grow up in ignorance and darkness, and all the moral and material helplessness which at present characterises their lives.

Plea for a Sympathetic Examination of the Whole Subject

'I will frankly confess that I have not introduced this resolution in the Council to-day in the hope that it will be adopted by the Council. Constituted as this body is, we all recognize that unless a resolution finds favour in the eyes of the Government, there is no chance of its being carried; and I recognize further that it is not reasonable to expect Government to accept this resolution without further consideration. Even if they are inclined to take a favourable view of my proposals, they are proposals which will naturally have to be referred to the Secretary of State before any decisive step is taken. I have not, therefore, the least expectation that this resolution will be adopted by the Council. But though the Government may not be able to accept the resolution, they certainly can undertake to examine the whole question at an early date in a sympathetic spirit. If that is done, I shall be satisfied. In any case, the Government, I trust, will not do two things. I trust that they will not make a definite pronouncement against the principle of free and compulsory education to-day; and I also trust that the resolution which I have moved will not be brushed aside on the plea that the condition of the finances does not admit of the proposals being maintained.

'There is much truth in the homely adage that where there is a will there is a way. I think that this question of free and compulsory primary education is now in this country the question of questions. The well-being of millions upon millions of children who are waiting to be brought under the humanising influence of education depends upon it. The increased efficiency of the individual, the higher general level of intelligence, the stiffening of the moral backbone of large sections of the community—none of these things can come without such education. In fact the whole of our future as a nation is inextricably bound up with it.

'However this resolution may be disposed of here to-day, I feel that in this matter we are bound to win. The practice of the whole civilised world, the sympathies of the British democracy, and our own natural and legitimate aspirations, of which Your Lordship has more than once admitted the reasonableness—all these are united in its favour. This resolution will come up again and again before this Council, till it is carried to a successful issue.

'I earnestly hope that the Government will read aright the needs of the situation, and not fail to move with the times in this matter. To my mind the call to them is clear, and it is also the call of statesmanship—that statesmanship which pursues, unhasting but unresting, the highest interests of the people committed to its care.'

This speech is a fine example of the crusading fervour which filled Mr. Gokhale, especially during the closing years of his life. The causes which he espoused, and especially the three great causes of elementary education, indentured labour, and the treatment of Indians in South Africa, became to him sacred issues to be pursued in a spirit of almost religious zeal. He perceived, in this instance, the vast wrong which was being done to many millions of his fellow-countrymen by the failure of the State to provide them with the rudiments of that enlightenment which would raise them towards a full manhood. He spoke for them as a champion of the weak and the dispossessed, determined that at all costs a great injustice should be swept away. The gravity with which he regarded the issue involved is shown by his declared willingness to increase the salt tax, which he hated so much, if no other means could be found of financing his project.

In no other respect has India more signally lost by Mr. Gokhale's premature death than in regard to elementary education. He was a man who could get things done. If he had been given a few more years of life there is no doubt that he would have carried this great reform. But no one has arisen to take up his mantle; and the cause of the children has found no efficient champion since he died.

XII

CLOSING YEARS

Gokhale's Elementary Education Bill

Early in 1911 Mr. Gokhale introduced his Elementary Education Bill into the Imperial Council. It was a cautious measure, of a merely permissive character and depending very largely upon local enthusiasm for the cause of education. In spite of strenuous efforts which he made in its behalf, including long tours through the country in order to educate public opinion, the Bill failed. Government professed themselves unable to find the money, and there was an unfortunate and short-sighted opposition to details of the measure from some of the non-official members in the Council.

Gokhale's last speech on the Bill concluded as follows —in words which are perhaps the noblest of all his public utterances:

'I know that my Bill will be thrown out before the day closes. I make no complaint. I shall not even be depressed. I know too well the story of the preliminary efforts that were required even in England, before the Act of 1870 was passed, either to complain or to feel depressed. Moreover, I have always felt and often said that we of the present generation in India can only hope to serve our country by our failures. The men and women who will be privileged to serve her by their successes will come later. We must be content to accept cheerfully the place that has been allotted to us in our onward march. This Bill, thrown out to-day, will come back again and again, till on the stepping-stones of its dead selves a measure ultimately rises which will spread the light of knowledge throughout the land. It may be that this anticipation will not come true. It may be that our efforts may not conduce even indirectly to the promotion of the great cause which we all have at heart, and that they may turn out after all to be nothing better than the mere ploughing of the sands of the sea-shore. But, My Lord, whatever fate awaits our labours one thing is clear. We shall be entitled to feel that we have done our duty; and, where the call of duty is clear, it is better even to labour and fail than not to labour at all.'

His Bill was thrown out, as he anticipated. He was the first great Indian to place in the forefront of his policy for his people's rebirth the necessity for the education of the common people; and in the words of Sir Valentine Chirol, he 'extracted nothing from official wisdom or parsimony but a frigid *non possumus*.'[1]

Police Administration

During the Council session of 1912 Mr. Gokhale made two important speeches, on matters concerning which he felt very deeply. The first was on the question of Police Administration, and contained references to what he, like many other Indian public men, had to endure in this connection. He had suffered much from the stupid suspicions harboured by the police in regard to his political activities. Mr. Ranade before his day had to submit to have his letters opened; he himself was well aware how all his movements were shadowed. What he and others had to bear in this connection the following passages relate:

'As a matter of fact I must say I have been receiving such attentions for a very long time, but I have always taken it as

[1] *India*, p. 153.

(all) in the day's work; and I am free to recognise that the Government may think it necessary to keep in touch with all who are engaged in such work. What we are entitled to expect, however, is that the men who are employed in this duty shall do their work in a less clumsy and offensive manner than that in which they do it at present. I will give the Council an illustration from my personal knowledge. I belong to a society of young men—I mean the other members are young men, though I am myself getting on in years—which has been brought into existence to supply a long-felt want, namely, that of young men trained in the study of public questions and engaged in public work in various fields as whole time workers. Now we may be right or we may be wrong in our view of things, in our estimate of the requirements of the situation. We have made up our minds to serve our country according to our lights, and we are prepared to accept the full consequences of our choice. And if the Criminal Investigation Department of the Government wishes to keep in touch with our movements, let it do so by all means; but we are certainly entitled, as peaceful citizens of this country, to expect that we should not be subjected to undue annoyance.

'Some time ago one of the members of our society went to the United Provinces to take part in the Famine Relief operations. He did such excellent work there in that connection that Sir John Hewett thought it necessary to recognise the work in his Famine Report; and yet this gentleman was subjected to such open and continuous annoyance by the men of the Criminal Investigation Department that ultimately he had to complain publicly of it in the papers. He was not only openly accompanied by these men wherever he went, but one of them began to go the length of insisting on sitting on the coach-box of hackney carriages engaged by him for going about.

'All this is really most grossly offensive—to put it no stronger than that. I do not say that they should not watch our movements, if they want to do so, though I strongly feel that it is most foolish that Government should thus let loose a number of unscrupulous men, such as most of the Criminal Investigation Department men are, on innocent people. But, in any case, it is necessary that all this shadowing should be done in a less offensive and less clumsy manner.

'The reports submitted by these men are secret. Nobody knows what is contained in these reports; and everybody's good name is at the mercy of these people. I know of a report which was once submitted against me, and for which there was absolutely no foundation. I came to know about it simply through the courtesy of the Political Secretary to the Bombay Government, who happened to entertain a kindly feeling for me. I had made a speech at a *mufussil* place in the Bombay Presidency. Some time after I happened to meet this officer at a party, and he asked me to go and see him the next day in his office. He then asked me what things I had been saying, and he put the report into my hands. I was amazed to read it. I told him that I had never said any of the things attributed to me. He laughed and said of course he knew that I could not have said such things and he never took the report seriously.

'This officer discredited the report because he knew me personally. But for one man whom these officers know personally, there are ten, a hundred, a thousand men whom they do not know, and against whom reports are daily submitted—reports on which officials very often act.

'It is therefore necessary that an enquiry should now be ordered into the operations of this Criminal Investigation Department. The fact is this: A number of uneducated and in many cases unscrupulous men have been engaged for this work. The work is necessarily regarded as disreputable, and is looked down upon in every society. A man who goes about it surreptitiously and tries to find out behind the backs of people something about them must necessarily suffer from that disadvantage. Therefore you cannot get good men for the work, and I recognise that that constitutes a serious difficulty; but some way must be found out of it, for great irritation and bitterness is being caused in the minds of thousands of innocent people by the dangerous and unscrupulous activity of the Criminal Investigation Department men.

'Therefore, an enquiry must now immediately be undertaken into the whole of this business—into how these men are appointed, what their qualifications are, how they perform their duties, what supervision there is on them, and what reliance is placed on their reports.

'The very fact that things are settling down again makes such an enquiry all the more necessary. For these men have to justify their existence, and therefore in the absence of anything really worth reporting they are sure to make up things which do not exist and report them to the Government.'

It was in this courageous and outspoken way that Mr. Gokhale drew attention to a grievance which has done more than anything else to alienate from Government the mind of modern educated India. The present writer can bear personal witness that, amongst Government officials, Gokhale himself, as Sir Valentine Chirol says, 'was generally regarded as a mere disaffected agitator, only the more dangerous, because of his admittedly greater ability.'[1]

Indentured Labour

In the same year, 1912, Mr. Gokhale made a noteworthy speech in defence of the Indentured Indian labourers in distant countries, on whose behalf his influence was destined to tell so decisively, and in whose ultimate liberation from a form of slavery he had so great and honourable a share.

'I do not think it necessary to describe to this Council at any length what this system really is. Its principal features may roughly be stated to be six in number. Under this system, those who are recruited bind themselves, first, to go to a distant and unknown land, the language, usages and customs of which they do not know, and where they have no friends or relatives. Secondly, they bind themselves to work there for any employer to whom they may be allotted, whom they do not know and who does not know them, and in whose

[1] *India*, p. 108.

choice they have no voice. Thirdly, they bind themselves to live there on the estate of the employer, they must not go anywhere without a special permit, and must do whatever tasks are assigned to them, no matter how irksome those tasks may be. Fourthly, the binding is for a certain fixed period, usually five years, during which time they cannot voluntarily withdraw from their contract and have no means of escaping from its hardships, however intolerable. Fifthly, they bind themselves to work during the period for a fixed wage, which invariably is lower, and in some cases very much lower, than the wage paid to free labour around them. And sixthly and lastly, and this to my mind is the worst feature of the system, they are placed under a special law, never explained to them before they left the country, which is in a language which they do not understand, and which imposes on them a criminal liability for the most trivial breaches of the contract, in place of the civil liability which usually attaches to such breaches. Thus they are liable under the law to imprisonment with hard labour, which may extend to two and in some cases to three months, not only for fraud, not only for deception, but for negligence, for carelessness, and—will the Council believe it?—for even an impertinent word or gesture to the manager or his overseers.

'These are the principal features of the system, and when it is remembered that the victims of the system—I can call them by no other name—are generally simple, ignorant, illiterate, resourceless people belonging to the poorest classes of this country, and that they are induced to enter—or it would be more correct to say, are entrapped into entering—into these agreements by the unscrupulous representations of wily, professional recruiters, who are paid so much a head for the labour they supply, and whose interest in them ceases the moment they are handed over to the emigration agents, no fair-minded man will, I think, hesitate to say that the system is a monstrous system, iniquitous in itself, based on fraud, and maintained by force; nor will he, I think, demur to the statement that a system so wholly opposed to modern sentiments of justice and humanity is a grave blot on the civilisation of any country that tolerates it.

The Objections to the Indenture System

'The principal objections to the system are roughly five. The first is naturally its utter inequity. Sir, whatever view one may take of the agreements into which these poor people are made to enter under the system, to dignify them by the name of "fair contract" is to misuse the English language. For the stream is poisoned at its very source. It is significant that nobody has a good word to say for the professional recruiters who entrap and entice away these poor people. The recruiters are admittedly men who are generally ignorant and unscrupulous, and who, with the exception of perhaps a very few, have never been to the Colonies for which they recruit, and who, being paid so much per head, try by hook or by crook to get into their meshes as many persons as they can. The Government of India stand aside on the plea that it is a fair contract between the emigrant and his future employer. How can a contract be called a fair contract, the two parties to which are most unequally matched? How can it be a fair contract when one party to it is absolutely in a state of ignorance and helplessness, and the other party—the powerful party—takes care that it shall not know how much it is undertaking to abide by? Take, for instance, the penal nature of the contract. The terms that are explained to the emigrants, when they enter into indenture, never include a statement of the penal nature of the law under which they have to live. Here in Volume III of the Sanderson Committee's report the Council will find the agreements for the different Colonies reproduced. There is not a word here about the penal liabilities thrown on the poor creatures by the special laws under which they must live in the several Colonies. If this single fact is explained to them before they agree to emigrate, namely, that they will be placed in the Colonies not under the ordinary Civil law for the enforcement of the contract, but under a special penal law rendering them liable to imprisonment with hard labour even for trivial faults, I should like to see how many even of such ignorant, resourceless people agree to go to these distant places.

'I say, therefore, that the stream is poisoned at the source; that it is not a fair contract: that it is a contract between two parties that are absolutely unequally matched, a contract vitiated by the fact that most important facts in connection with it are kept from the knowledge of one party.

Lack of Efficient Safeguards

'The apologists of the system, however, urge that there are safeguards provided to prevent hardship and injustice to the emigrants when they go to their respective colonies. Two such safeguards are specially mentioned. One is that in every colony there is an officer, known as the Protector of Immigrants, specially to look after the interests of indentured immigrants. And, secondly, there are the magistrates to give the protection of the law to the immigrants against any cruelty that may be practised on them by their employers.

'These safeguards look all right on paper; in actual practice, however, both are found to be more or less illusory. These men—the protectors and the magistrates—are officers of the Colonial Governments. They belong to the same class to which the planters belong. They are generally one in sympathy and in interests with the planters; and it is not in ordinary human nature that they should care to displease those with whom they have to live, with whom they have to mix socially—and all this for granting protection to poor, ignorant people from a distant land, in whom their interest is purely official.

The Suffering under the System

'My third objection to this system is the vast and terrible amount of suffering that it has caused during the 75 years that it has been in existence. It is difficult to speak in terms of due restraint on this point. Even the hardest heart must melt to think of this phase of the question. I will not speak now of the imprisonments with hard labour endured for trivial faults; I will not speak of the personal violence which in some cases has been proved, and in very many cases could not be proved, though alleged. I will not speak of the bitterness engendered in the minds of thousands when they realised that they had been deceived, that they had been entrapped, and that there was no escape for them. I will not speak of the homesick feeling, destroying their interest in life. These are all serious matters that could be charged against the system. But more serious even than these is the heavy mortality that has prevailed in the past in all Colonies under the system, a mortality which has been examined from time to time by Commissions of Inquiry, and which has been established beyond doubt—a mortality for which indentured emigration was prohibited to the Federated Malay States only last year, and which even to-day is admitted to exist in certain districts of Assam amongst the statute labourers.

'Then the numerous suicides which have resulted from this system—poor innocent people preferring death by their own hands to life under it—are a ghastly feature of the system.

'All this constitutes a sum total of human misery which is appalling to contemplate, and which will be a standing witness against the system for all time. It is true that things are somewhat better now; but they cannot be very much better under a system which has inherent characteristics such as those that I have described. Moreover, as Lord Curzon said in this Council in 1901, even if such cases have occurred only in a few instances, the very fact that such cases can occur under the system constitutes a severe condemnation of the system.

'My fourth objection to the system is the frightful immorality that is inseparable from it. This is a fact which has been admitted by everybody, among others by the Government of India and by the Sanderson Committee. The committee, who deal with all other phases of the indenture question, carefully avoid making any recommendation as to how the frightful immorality involved in the system may be remedied. Under the law, every hundred male indentured labourers must be accompanied by 40 females. Now very few respectable women can be got to go these long distances. Our men themselves do not really care to go, much less do the women. The statutory number, therefore, is made up by the recruiters, as admitted by the Government of India in one of their despatches to the Secretary of State, by including in it women of admittedly loose morals, with results in the Colonies which one had better leave to the imagination of the Council than describe. . . .

A National Degradation

'My last objection to the system is that it is degrading to the people of India from a national point of view. I do not think I need really say much on this aspect of the question. Wherever the system exists, there the Indians are only known as coolies, no matter what their position may be. Now, Sir, there are disabilities enough in all conscience attaching to our position in this country. And, I ask, why must this additional brand be put upon our brow before the rest of the civilised world? I am sure, if only the Government will exercise a little imagination, and realise our feeling in the matter, it will see the necessity of abolishing the system as soon as possible. . . .

The Responsibility of Government

'This is a question which really throws a great responsibility upon the Government. I am aware that the Government of India have from time to time taken up the position that they maintain an attitude of neutrality in this matter, that they do not themselves encourage indentured emigration, but that if people choose to accept certain terms and go, it is not for them to interfere. I would only ask the Council to contrast this attitude with the attitude which the Govenment have adopted in regard to the peasantry of the country, in legislating on lines to which I have already referred. I do not think that the Government can absolve themselves from their responsibility in this matter. In the first place, the recruiters are granted licenses to recruit by District magistrates. That, in itself, imposes a responsibility upon the Government, because by granting licenses to these persons the Government make themselves to a certain extent responsible for the representations by which these men secure recruits. Then, the magistrates before whom the poor emigrants are taken and made to enter into agreements are the servants of Government. The third and last point is that, though the fact about the penal nature of the contract has been carefully kept out of all agreements all these years, the Government have so far taken no steps whatever to remedy this. . . .

'If you are prepared to abolish the penal nature of the contract under which these labourers have to work, the rest would be comparatively a very simple question, and I shall not press this motion to a division; but, as I understand it, the penal provisions are the very essence of the system; without them the system cannot be worked. If penal liability is thus indispensable, I ask why the Government have not taken steps all these years to see to it that this nature of the contract is explained to the emigrants before they enter into their agreements? Sir, this is really a most serious question; for, whatever the Government may say, as a matter of fact everybody in the country believes that without the countenance of Government the system could not have gone on so long.

'India is the only country which supplies indentured labour at the present moment. Why should India be marked out for this degradation? The conscience of our people, unfortunately asleep too long, is now waking up to the enormity of this question; and I have no doubt that it will not rest till it has asserted itself. And I ask the Government not to make the mistake of ignoring a sentiment that is dear to us, namely the sentiment of our self-respect. We have no doubt plenty of differences between the Government and the people in regard to the internal administration of this country; but those are matters which stand on a different footing. Outside the country, the Government of India must stand up for us on every occasion, must stand up for our dignity, for our honour, for our national pride. If they will not do this, to whom else can we turn?

'I feel that though this system has been allowed to exist so long, yet its days are really numbered. It will soon cease in Assam, and then it cannot last very much longer in the case of the Colonies. And I am confident that a people who have spent millions upon millions in emancipating slaves, will not long permit their own fellow-subjects to be condemned to a life which, if not one of actual slavery, is at any rate not far removed from it. . . .

'The Government, it is clear, are not going to accept this

Resolution: that being so, the Resolution is bound to be thrown out. But that will not be the end of the matter. This motion, the Council may rest assured, will be brought forward again and again, till we carry it to a successful issue. It affects our national self-respect; and therefore the sooner the Government recognise the necessity of accepting it, the better it will be for all parties.'

Work for Indians in South Africa

This great speech on behalf of a voiceless multitude of his exiled fellow-countrymen places Gokhale in the ranks of that noble fellowship of the enemies of slavery, which includes the names of Wilberforce, of Clarkson, and of Garrison. Gokhale's sympathy did not stop at words. Although his health was at the time very unsatisfactory, he sailed for South Africa in 1912—at the invitation of Mr. M. K. Gandhi, and with the sanction and encouragement of the Colonial Office and the Indian Government—in order to seek some means of redressing the grievances of Indians, indentured and otherwise, in that country. The reception accorded to him was excellent, and he succeeded in securing from the South African authorities the promise of better treatment for Indians in a variety of particulars. After his return to India, however, further difficulties arose, which led to the famous passive resistance campaign organised by Mr. Gandhi. Gokhale was immensely interested in this movement, and undertook a very strenuous campaign of public meetings up and down India in order to raise funds, and to educate public opinion in its support. The present writer will never forget the power and eloquence with which the great patriot addressed one of these meetings at Delhi, where he was in the audience.

Closing Years

THE PUBLIC SERVICES COMMISSION

The strain of this campaign was however very severe, and it was incurred at a time when Mr. Gokhale's energies were also heavily engaged in the work of the Public Services Commission, of which he had been made a member. This Commission had been appointed 'to consider the claims of Indians to higher and more extensive employment in the public service connected with the civil administration of the country.' At the time when the appointment of the Commission had first been mooted, Gokhale had propounded four tests by which it might be estimated whether or no the Government of India was genuinely progressive, namely, first the attention paid to the moral and material improvement of the people; second, the pains taken to foster the development of local self-government; third, the degree to which the principle of representative government was in force in the legislatures; and fourth, the extent to which Indians were admitted into the ranks of the public service. He saw considerable signs of advance in regard to the first three of these four standards, but very little in regard to the fourth.

The work of the Public Services Commission proved to be very arduous, and his strength was failing. He did not live to see the completion of its task. Gokhale complained of the deep-seated prejudices with which the official witnesses were filled; the evidence given by such witnesses was little but a continuous cry of Indian incapacity. He told his friends at the Servants of India Society that he never had to undergo such severe mental strain as during this period. Six hours a day were spent in the hearing of evidence in public, and many hours had also to be spent on the studying of written statements. The strain was more than his weakened physique could stand. 'His already over-worked system had combated with an enormous amount of public work of a very anxious character; and the South African affair was drawing his heart's best blood. For this fresh duty he practically worked through all the twenty-four hours of the day. Even his dinner and recreation hour was given to some discussion or other in relation to this great question. He was always a light sleeper; and the anxiety and mental strain deprived him even of the little sleep he was accustomed to enjoy. Often in the dead of night he was heard pacing up and down his room, with half articulate utterances, showing his deeply absorbed state of mind.'[1]

The Indian Cause in South Africa

His doctors, both in India and in Europe, gave him clear warning of what would follow if he did not relax the strain. But he felt the issues involved in the work of the Public Services Commission to be worth every sacrifice he could make; and he never ceased his crusade on behalf of his suffering fellow-countrymen in South Africa, and in the other Colonies where the system of indenture was in vogue. In this great cause his efforts were ably seconded by Mr. C. F. Andrews, and he had the good fortune to find a sympathetic helper and adviser in the person of Lord Hardinge; with the result that not long after Gokhale's death the evil system which had perpetuated for so long the spirit of slavery was brought to an end. In spite of the yeoman service done in the cause by other leaders, this triumph must primarily be regarded as won by Gokhale himself.

[1] Shahani, *op. cit.*, p. 197.

How much these various cares oppressed him and how deeply he felt in regard to them is indicated by a letter written from England in May, 1913.

'The pressure of work and engagements has much increased during the last fortnight; and the ear-specialist whom I saw this morning expressed his serious disappointment that it should be so. My ear has now improved a good deal—about half the normal hearing has returned; but he thinks that further improvement is possible, only I must have no work or engagements of any kind for about six months more. This is, as you will see, an impossible condition, and I must do the best I can in the circumstances. Already the prospect of a renewal of the South African struggle is hanging over my head like a sword. For if our countrymen find it necessary to resume passive resistance, I *must* return to India in time for the September Session of the Council, and raise a debate at Simla on the whole question. And then we must do what we can to organise assistance for the cause throughout the country. This is extremely unfortunate from the standpoint of my health; for I don't quite know how far I shall be able to bear that strain in my present state. However I feel there is no choice in the matter, and I must take what comes.

'I have sent a long telegram to Polak this week, in which I have suggested to him that he should come here as soon as passive resistance is resumed, and that after re-organising the London Committee (which is moribund at present) he and I should go together to India at the end of August. If he is by my side in India, the strain on me will be far less. I saw Lord Ampthill last Tuesday, and we have arranged to raise a debate in the House of Lords on the question at an early date. Our difficulty just now is that we are not yet in possession of all the amendments which have been accepted in the Union Parliament. We hope to get that information to-morrow.'

Gokhale and Gandhi

Mr. Polak, however, who was closely associated with Mr. Gandhi in this cause of the Indians in South Africa, went to prison along with his leader instead of coming to India as Gokhale desired. When the conflict came to an end with the Gandhi-Smuts agreement in 1914 Gokhale was in India once more. He was able to receive Gandhi at the Servants of India Home on his return in triumph, and to show his unflagging interest in the cause of his oppressed countrymen. But his strength was visibly ebbing. Did he realise that this was the man who more than any other individual was to take his place in the national struggle? We have seen how greatly Gandhi honoured Gokhale. What Gokhale thought of his younger contemporary he has left on record:

'In all my life I have known only two men who have affected me spiritually in the manner that Gandhi does—our great patriarch, Mr. Dadabhai Naoroji, and my late master, Mr. Ranade, men before whom not only are we ashamed of doing anything unworthy but in whose presence our very minds are afraid of thinking anything that is unworthy.'

Mr. Natarajan has described a scene when, during the last weeks of his life, Gokhale took him and another leading Indian into his confidence, in regard to difficulties that had arisen between the Viceroy, Lord Hardinge, and Mr. Gandhi as to the right procedure to be followed in support of the Indian cause in South Africa. The Viceroy, while strongly upholding that cause, was at variance with Mr. Gandhi as to the right course to pursue; and Gokhale had the task of bringing about agreement.

'Mr. Gokhale,' Mr. Natarajan relates, 'was much distressed. We could see that the difficulty of mediating between these two personages was severely straining his fast failing health.'[1]

'The Other Side'

The arduous work done by Gokhale in 1913 and 1914 for the cause of Indians in South Africa and in connection with the Public Services Commission led to a rapid increase in the diabetic trouble from which he had been suffering for a number of years. The closing weeks of his life were rendered uneasy by a controversy amongst the leaders of the Indian National Congress regarding the Congress 'Creed' or statement of political aims and objects. Gokhale and other leaders of the Moderate group wished this creed to include a plain statement that the policy of the Congress was that of attaining self-government by constitutional means within the British Empire. They also introduced a clause regulating the appointment of delegates to the Congress; this did not find acceptance with the leaders of the more extreme party in the Congress. The controversy which arose proved very distressing to Gokhale in his weakened state of health.

Early in 1915 it became obvious that his condition was very serious, and on February 19th he died. To his comrades of the Servants of India Society who were by his side at the end he said, in Marathi, 'This side of life has been good to me. It is time that I should go and see the other.'

[1] Natarajan, *op. cit.*, p. 6

XIII

GOKHALE'S PLACE IN HISTORY

IT is an interesting coincidence—and perhaps more than a coincidence—that Lord Morley turned straight from his first interview with Gokhale to a renewed study of Cavour.[1] The essential similarity between the minds of the two men may have exercised an influence, if only sub-consciously, upon the thoughts of the great and wise Liberal statesman. For in studying the career and the spirit of Gokhale one is constantly reminded of Cavour.

The setting of the two statesmen's lives was of course entirely different. The Italian had the nucleus of a free Piedmont from which to start in his liberation of Italy. He had his ten years of office as minister in a responsible government. He had countless opportunities for taking, by his own choice, decisions which were of far-reaching practical importance in the actual work of nation-building. Gokhale had none of these advantages. He started and he remained a citizen of an India under alien control. He was always in opposition. He never had an adequate opportunity (except in minor affairs, such as in connection with the Poona Municipality) to prove that he possessed the gifts of the administrator and the legislator. He died before his unceasing labour had borne fruit in the creation of a system under which

[1] Morley, *Reminiscences*, vol. II, p. 139.

the chosen representatives of the Indian people can bear the responsibilities of office.

None the less, there is an essential similarity between Cavour and Gokhale, because the two men had the same political purpose and ideal—the same determination to use what they had in their hands to the fullest advantage in order to gain more. They were both 'masters of the possible,' setting before themselves limited objectives, using existing machinery, however defective, for the attainment of those objectives; and when they were attained, going forward, one step more, to some other practical and limited objective. Both of them were given by fate only a few years of greatness—and by a curious coincidence this period was in both cases that of thirteen years—but in so short a time, by their practical policy of using existing resources to the utmost for limited ends, they each of them achieved immense successes. They were both inherently constitutionalists—that is, men who perceived that revolutionary methods, even if they succeed for a time in realising the popular will, have, as their inevitable ultimate result, a reaction which may carry things backward almost as far as the first starting point. In consequence, both of them were anathema to the hot-heads in their respective lands. The Mazzinians hated Cavour worse even than they hated the Austrians, and it is perhaps true that the Indian 'Extremists' hated Gokhale worse even than they hated the British.

In consequence Gokhale has not yet come into his own. His countrymen even now regard him as a faint-hearted 'Moderate,' who was willing to take what he could get, and to use the weapons which were put into his hands by his opponents. Probably another generation will have to pass—and what is a generation in the long stream of Indian history?—before it begins to be recognised how immense were the benefits which this college professor conferred upon his Motherland. For years he stood forth, in the eyes both of the Indian Government and of the British democracy, as *the* representative Indian. In his person it was proved possible that India should take the gift of democratic institutions in government, and use that gift wisely and sanely for the building up of a sound national life. For years the reactionaries could be met with the convincing words, 'But look at Gokhale: here at any rate is a man who is obviously a statesman of genius, prepared to accept and to work constitutionally the gift of responsible government.' The reactionaries did not always agree. The present writer has a vivid memory of using some such words to an English officer in a remote district, about the year 1913, and of being met with the contemptuous assertion that Gokhale was merely 'a seditionist in disguise.' But the best men amongst the officials realised something of Gokhale's real greatness, and of his significance both for India and the Empire.

Of those who came into direct contact with Gokhale in the work of the Legislature, the lesser men believed and trembled; the big men—men of the stamp of Morley, Minto and Hardinge—accepted with gladness the fact that here was an Indian leader fit to be ranked by the side of the great constructive statesmen of the world, with a definite programme in view for his country's future, and with concise and concrete policies in mind whereby he might reach his objective.

For the uniqueness of Gokhale lay largely in this: that he did not merely criticise and abuse the Government, and leave it at that, as so many of his Indian opponents were—and are still—inclined to do. He saw the shortcomings of the existing system as clearly as anyone. He was instant in season and out of season at the task of pointing out those shortcomings. *But he was always constructive.* He always had a better method to suggest in individual cases of mal-administration; and in regard to broad general principles, he knew exactly what the next step ought to be, and where the deficiencies of things, as they were, called most urgently for practical redress.

So much was this so, that Gokhale ceased, during his later years of greatness, to be merely a leader of opposition. Technically he remained such; but in fact he became a leader—and in some relations almost a dictator—of the best elements in Government policy. His moral stature was so commanding, his personal ascendancy became so marked, that men of enlightenment and goodwill who found themselves responsible for directing the destinies of the Indian people were glad to accept his guidance wherever they could. Thus it came about that his advice had such a far-reaching effect in regard to the Minto-Morley reforms; that his crusade on behalf of indentured labour succeeded in wiping out that shameful survival of the epoch of slavery; that his recommendations in the great Budget speeches had year after year decisive effect in shaping the financial policy of Government; that his unceasing advocacy of the Indianisation of the Services eventually bore definite fruit; that after his death much of what he had striven for was achieved in the Montagu-Chelmsford Reforms; and that in a great number of other particulars his practical idealism was justified by the formation of enlightened policies and definite measures of reform. It is true that some of his battles are not yet won, notably those in regard to free and universal education, to expenditure on the army, and to the treatment of Indians in South Africa. Nor is 'the self-determination of India,' of which he dreamed, yet a reality. But in relation to these causes he initiated a movement which quite evidently can never cease till his ends are attained. 'The stars in their courses fight for him'; and though he is dead, his spirit lives on in the continual progress of such liberal movements towards their destined success.

Gokhale was above all else a champion of the poor and helpless. The unlettered peasants, the indentured coolies pining for their home-country, the victims of ignorance, exploitation, oppression, called him to an endless and zealous championship which wore him out in their service. He struggled for his country's rights primarily because he felt her to be weak and oppressed. For him nationalism was a sane and steady force for the righting of wrongs. He was a nationalist because he was a humanitarian, a friend of the helpless, a tribune of the common people. He cared nothing for personal advantage. He refused a knighthood; he refused a place on the Secretary of State's Council. He did all his work for his country in the spirit in which he had taken up his first post under the Deccan Education Society, the spirit which thinks first and always of the need to be met, and which sacrifices all personal considerations to the meeting of that need.

The problems of the contact between East and West have never been more urgent than they are to-day. From the beginning there have been two streams of thought and activity in evidence on both sides of this world-problem. In the West there has been the spirit of exploitation, of conquest, of dominance—the spirit whose most obvious and naked embodiment was seen in the African slave-trade, but which has shown itself in all lands where the contact has taken place, whether in isolated acts of frightfulness or in settled systems. On the other hand there has been the spirit of brotherhood, expressing itself through the sense of national responsibility evinced in the trial of Warren Hastings, in the later revisions of the Charter of the East India Company, and in the Royal Declaration of 1858; and also through the great agencies, such as the enterprise of Christian Missions, which seek to give, rather than to rule or to get, in their relations with the East.

Correspondingly there has been a double spirit in evidence in the East. The Western spirit of dominance and of exploitation has led to the creation of a spirit of intransigence, of extremism, of determination to take nothing by way of a favour, but to boycott and to non-co-operate. On the other hand the better spirit of the West has found an echo in such men as Gokhale, who are willing to take all that is given, and to use it strenuously, and in constructive co-operation with the Western rulers in order that the highest good of the country may be attained.

From this point of view Gokhale is an emblem of the brightest hope for the future contact of East and West, and therefore for the future of humanity. He stands for the fact that West and East—or the best elements in either—can come together in a spirit of goodwill, and can co-operate for the good of mankind. He shows that the great achievement of the West, liberal methods of government, can be understood, grasped and used by the East, for the carrying through of a thousand measures of emancipation and enlightenment.

Hence Gokhale is a beacon of immense hopefulness for the future. One man such as Gokhale is enough to refute a thousand prophets of woe, who foretell catastrophe if Western methods of government are transplanted to the East. His speeches and the records of his life should be read and re-read by everyone who is anxious to understand the problem of the relationships between England and India, or is interested in the vast enterprise of naturalising Western methods of government in the East.

Gokhale had many faults to find with the British system in India; but he himself was, in truth, the most striking of all proofs of the fact that in the main this system has been successful. Methods of education, of local and national government, of Imperial relationship, which in the end produced this great man—even if they had never produced any other great men—are thereby proved not to have existed altogether in vain. They have borne their fruit in him, and in the spirit which he embodied; and it is a noble fruit.

Finally, behind all Gokhale's activities, behind his deliberate sacrifice of his leisure, his health, and in the end his life, for the sake of his country, behind his unswerving resolution to take the best which the West has to offer and use it for the uplifting and the emancipation of the East, lay a deep realisation of the meaning of our common humanity. This expressed itself, not only in his work for the downtrodden and the distressed, but in those appeals which he uttered from time to time, and always with such deep feeling, that England should remember her best self, and act generously and with sympathy by India. He had a profound confidence in the underlying kinship of humanity, both East and West, and in the fact that an appeal to the better nature, even of the governing power, would call forth a due response.[1]

This is indeed the last word which is to be said concerning the relations of England and India—that there should be sympathy and generosity, a willingness to trust, a belief in the healing and moderating influence of liberty. Gokhale stands, and will stand (though we are not as yet far enough away from him to discern his true greatness) as, above all, a Reconciler. He takes the best that there is in the West, to interpret it and use it for the good of the East. He turns to the West, as spokesman of the longings and aspirations of the East, appealing above all for brotherhood. With his great natural powers and force of character he might have ridden the whirlwind, denouncing the iniquities of the West, and telling a people always ready to listen to such appeals that they must separate themselves from all these abominations. Had he chosen such a course, immense popularity would have been his. He need not then have worn himself to death in the effort to adapt and transform Western institutions. But he chose the harder path, that of the Unifier, the Reconciler; and it is only as it is considered in this light that the true greatness of his work will be appreciated.

He was a great 'master of the possible,' a constructive statesman of the first rank, a bringer-together of East and West in the common service of the needy; above all an idealist, a foreseer, a prophet of a new era of inter-racial goodwill and co-operation.

[1] In this connection it is interesting to notice the earnest appeal for sympathetic treatment of India by England made by the present King Emperor, and recorded in Lord Morley's *Reminiscences*, vol. II.

APPENDIX

GOKHALE'S POLITICAL TESTAMENT

IN 1914, at the instance of a distinguished Provincial Governor, Gokhale prepared a scheme of Reforms to be inaugurated by the Government of their own accord in order to avoid the growing discontent in the country.[1] The scheme was entrusted to H.H. the Aga Khan, by whom it was published in 1917. It is of interest as embodying Gokhale's conceptions of the next step that should be taken towards his ideal of a fully self-governing India, and also as affording certain grounds of comparison and contrast with the Montagu-Chelmsford Reforms of 1919, and with later constitutional developments upon which his influence is clearly visible.

PROVINCIAL AUTONOMY

The grant of Provincial Autonomy foreshadowed in the Delhi Despatch would be a fitting concession to make to the people of India at the close of the War. This will involve the two-fold operation of freeing the Provincial Governments on one side from the greater part of the control which is at present exercised over them by the Government of India and the Secretary of State in connection with the internal administration of the country, and substituting on the other, in place of the control so removed, the control of the representatives of tax-payers through Provincial Legislative Councils. I indicate below in brief outline the form of administration

[1] See a statement to the Press by the Hon. Mr. V. S. Srinivasa Shastri (President of the Servants of India Society) printed in *Indian Reforms* (Natesan).

that should be set up in different Provinces to carry out this idea.

Each Province should have:

(1) A Governor appointed from England at the head of the administration.

(2) A Cabinet or Executive Council of six members, three of whom should be Englishmen and three Indians, with the following portfolios:

- (*a*) Home (including Law and Justice).
- (*b*) Finance.
- (*c*) Agriculture, Irrigation and Public Works.
- (*d*) Education.
- (*e*) Local Self-Government (including Sanitation and Medical Relief).
- (*f*) Industries and Commerce.

While members of the Indian Civil Service should be eligible for appointment to the Executive Council, no place in the Council should be reserved for them, the best men available being taken, both English and Indian.

(3) A Legislative Council of between 75 and 100 members, of whom not less than four-fifths should be elected by different constituencies and interests. Thus in the Bombay Presidency, roughly speaking, each district should return two members, one representing Municipalities and the other District and Taluka Boards. The City of Bombay should have about ten members allotted to it. Bodies in the mofussil like the Karachi Chamber, the Ahmedabad mill-owners, the Deccan Sardars, should have a member each. Then there would be the special representation of Muhammadans, and here and there a member may have to be given to communities like the Lingayats, where they are strong. There should be no nominated non-official members, except as experts. A few official members may be added by the Governor as experts, or to assist in representing the Executive Government.

(4) The relations between the Executive Government and the Legislative Council so constituted should be roughly similar to those between the Imperial Government and the Reichstag in Germany. The Council will have to pass all Provincial legislation, and its assent will be necessary for

additions to or changes in Provincial taxation. The Budget, too, will have to come to it for discussion, and its resolutions in connection with it, as also on questions of general administration, will have to be given effect to unless vetoed by the Governor. More frequent meetings or longer continuous sittings will also have to be provided for. But the members of the Executive Government shall not depend, individually or collectively, on the support of a majority of the Council, for holding their offices.

The Provincial Government, so reconstituted and working under the control of the Legislative Council, as outlined above, should have complete charge of the internal administration of the Province, and it should have virtually independent financial powers, the present financial relations between it and the Government of India being largely revised—and to some extent even reversed. The revenue under Salt, Customs, Tributes, Railways, Post, Telegraphs and Mint should belong exclusively to the Government of India, the services being Imperial: while that under Land Revenue, including Irrigation, Excise, Forests, Assessed Taxes, Stamps and Registration should belong to the Provincial Governments, the services being Provincial. As under this division the revenue falling to the Provincial Governments will be in excess of their existing requirements, and that assigned to the Government of India will fall short of its present expenditure, the Provincial Governments should be required to make an annual contribution to the Government of India fixed for periods of five years at a time. Subject to this arrangement the Imperial and the Provincial Governments should develop their separate systems of finance, the Provincial Governments being given powers of taxation and borrowing within certain limits.

Such a scheme of Provincial Autonomy will be incomplete unless it is accompanied by (*a*) a liberalising of the present form of District administration, and (*b*) a great extension of Local Self-Government. For (*a*) it will be necessary to abolish the Commissionerships of Divisions, except where special reasons may exist for their being maintained, as in Sind, and to associate small District Councils, partly elected and partly nominated, with the Collector, to whom most of the present powers of the Commisioners could then be transferred—the functions of the (District) Councils being advisory to begin with. And (*b*) Villlage Panchayats, partly elected and partly nominated, should be created for villages and groups of villages and Municipal Boards in towns and Taluka Boards. The Talukas should be made wholly elected bodies, the Provincial Government reserving to itself, and exercising, stringent powers of control. A portion of the excise revenue should be made over to those bodies, so that they may have adequate resources at their disposal for the due performance of their duties. The District being too large an area for efficient Local Self-Government by an honorary agency, the functions of the District Board should be strictly limited, and the Collector should continue to be its ex-officio President.

The Government of India

The Provinces being thus rendered practically autonomous, the constitution of the Executive Council or the Cabinet of the Viceroy will have to be correspondingly altered. At present there are four members in that Council with portfolios which concern the internal administration of the country, namely, Home, Agriculture, Education and Industries and Commerce. As all internal administration will now be made over to Provincial Governments, and the Government of India will only retain in its hands nominal control to be exercised on very rare occasions, one member, to be called Member for the Interior, should suffice in place of these four. It will, however, be necessary to create certain other portfolios; and I would have the Council consist of the following six members, at least two of whom shall always be Indians:

(*a*) Interior.
(*b*) Finance.
(*c*) Law.
(*d*) Defence.
(*e*) Communications (Railway, Post and Telegraph).
(*f*) Foreign.

The Legislative Council of the Viceroy should be styled the Legislative Assembly of India. Its members should be raised to about one hundred to begin with, and its powers enlarged, but the principle of an official majority (for which perhaps it will suffice to substitute a nominated majority) should for the present be maintained, until sufficient experience has been gathered of the working of autonomous arrangements for the provinces. This will give the Government of India a reserve power in connection with provincial administration to be exercised in emergencies. Thus if a Provincial Legislative Council persistently decline to pass legislation which the Government regard as essential in the vital interests of the Province, it could be passed by the Government of India in its Legislative Assembly over the head of the Province. Such occasions would be extremely rare; but the reserve power will give a sense of security to the authorities, and will induce them to enter on the great experiment of Provincial Autonomy with greater readiness. Subject to this principle of an official or nominated majority being for the present maintained, the Assembly should have increased opportunities of influencing the policy of the Government by discussion, questions connected with the Army and Navy (to be now created) being placed on a level with other questions. In fiscal matters the Government of India so constituted should be freed from the control of the Secretary of State, whose control in other matters, too, should be largely reduced, his Council being abolished and his position steadily approximated to that of the Secretary of State for the Colonies.

Commissions in the Army and Navy must now be given to Indians with proper facilities for military and naval instruction.

German East Africa, if conquered from the Germans, should be reserved for Indian colonisation, and should be handed over to the Government of India.

INDEX